To : Belove

With gratitude !

Janice

BLOOM

STORIES FOR WOMEN TO NURTURE YOUR
GROWTH AND WATER YOUR SOUL

Chapter 12

BLOOM: Stories for Women to Nurture your Growth and Water Your Soul Vol.1

ISBN: 978-0-578-76353-8

Dedication

To my nieces, Ciarra and Cheri. To their daughters, Caila, Taylor, and Kennedy. And to the daughters of generations to come. I dedicate this book to you.

Table of Contents

Acknowledgements

To my AMAZING contributing authors. Words cannot express the depth of gratitude I have for each of you. Thank you for believing in the vision and for the excellence you brought to this project. Because of you, women around the world will be inspired to live their life in full bloom.

To my business mentor and friend, Trevor Otts. You are an extraordinary trailblazer. The supportive vision you provided for this project took BLOOM to a whole new level. Thank you for your commitment to helping us succeed.

To Jaime Washington, my publishing coach. Thank you for being a heart-centered coach who cares deeply for her clients. You took on this project with great enthusiasm and dedication. I am forever grateful for the selfless support I received from you and your team.

To my parents, James and Queenester Reynolds; and to my sisters, Cassandra and Michele Reynolds. You are the foundation on which I stand. I am secure in knowing that you will always be there for me.

To the women who sit on the front row of my life: Angel Townsend, Barbara Patterson, and Kathy Paige. Thank you for always celebrating and lifting me. With every word and every action, you demonstrate the power of true friendship.

"Now to Him who is able to do far more abundantly than all that we ask or think, according to the power at work within us, (Ephesians 3:20). For without You I can do nothing. Thank you, Lord, for entrusting me with this vision. May this work bring great glory and honor to Your name.

1

Foreword

I am a middle-aged successful entrepreneur. I have owned several businesses over the years. Entrepreneurship has been my primary focus since I hit the glass ceiling in Corporate America in my mid-thirties. A ceiling that seemed predetermined to limit my success within its walls. Despite having an education from Harvard Business School, having traveled the world to eight continents, and having led billion-dollar project initiatives, I have still found myself having to rebloom every few years. I have learned that no amount of success guarantees happiness, and no amount of happiness guarantees there will not be stumbling blocks along its path. With blooming, I have come to expect the thorns that surround it.

The reason I am so drawn to BLOOM is the raw transparency of the stories from the twenty brave women within it. BLOOM is revealing and transformative. It is timely, and it is priceless. BLOOM may most of all be a collection of bravery and inspiration by unapologetic women who dare to face adversity, clarity, their truth, and push through whatever confronts them to a season of blooming. BLOOM is so meaningful because the journeys are revealing and truthful. They are never linear outcomes but often jagged, two steps backward and sideways.

Sheila Reynolds has navigated this body of work to a collection of herstories. We are taken on an open and transparent journey of discovery, enlightenment, struggle, pain, rejection, and sometimes redemption. We have the unique opportunity to sit side-saddle as these women share their indirect paths to blooming. We will find ourselves cheering for these ladies, praying for them, crying with them, and for them, as each of these talented women unpack their tried and tested pathways. Most astonishing is their willingness to strip away the layers of pain, betrayal, and injustice some experienced while not giving up.

BLOOM may just become a blueprint for reaching one's "created" potential. BLOOM does not disappoint in offering a collection of breadcrumbs for those seeking wisdom, lessons learned, and teachable moments.

I am pleased to call Sheila, my friend, my shero, and a fellow author. Her inspiration for this book allows us to see the magic behind the curtain. It provides to those who read this body of work is priceless, and might I say simply unforgettable to achieve BLOOMing.

La Detra White President and CEO, Noble Insight

To learn more about La Detra White, please visit her website: www.ladetrawhite.com.

Introduction

There is nothing more beautiful than flowers in full bloom! The magnificence and splendor produced from a tiny seed growing up from the dirt, gaining strength over time to break through, bud, blossom and BLOOM is amazing. This complex and phenomenal evolution of a flower reflects the stories told in this book.

BLOOM: Stories For Women To Nurture Your Growth and Water Your Soul is a celebration of the evolution of "grown" and accomplished women who decided not just to live, but BLOOM and, at the same time, help others do the same. It is a sneak peek into the lives of 20 influential, high achieving women who candidly share the circumstances they found themselves "planted in" and the journey of choices made, both good and bad, that allowed them to rise through the dirt of life and BLOOM into the beautiful and uniquely designed person they were created to be.

Their stories provide a proven roadmap to success, coupled with practical wisdom, often only learned after years of trials and error. These powerful women, now in the prime of their lives, present this to you as a bouquet of flowers in book format, full of transformative stories and lessons that won't wilt, but have lasting impact and beauty for generations to come.

So, grab a cup of coffee, lounge back in your favorite chair, and let your soul be watered and refreshed.

SHEILA REYNOLDS

A red rose symbolizes love, respect, admiration and devotion.

"As the rose represents love in its various forms, my life reflects the beauty of the greatest Love of all who lives in me, who loves through me, who heals through me. I give Him the highest honor of all, Jesus Christ, My Lord."

Chapter 1

The Journey Back To Me
Sheila D. Reynolds

Who gets married for the first time at forty-five years old and then divorced at fifty? Especially a woman who wanted to be married ever since she could remember and who held marriage in the highest regard. She was a woman who waited, kept herself, and was determined to be the best wife possible. She didn't believe in divorce and was puzzled as to why two Christians couldn't just "work it out." So, when her marriage ended five short years into a lifetime, she was shocked.

That woman is me. Sheila Denise Reynolds. Someone I knew so well, yet a time came in my life where I wondered where she'd gone.

The Sheila I Knew

I was an ambitious, confident, and independent woman with an unquenchable fire for God. My life was devoted to studying the Bible, praying, and serving the church through teaching and loving God's people. I was especially passionate about mentoring young women, helping them reach their highest potential, both spiritually and professionally. I was a leader who led by example and approached life with optimism. I became well respected as a woman with high standards and integrity.

Like the exquisite beauty of a rose, I was a woman in full BLOOM.

Friends and admirers would ask, "Do you ever want to get married?" I would be puzzled with surprise. Of course, I do! Thinking to myself, "What kind of question is that? I've ALWAYS wanted to be married!" But did I? There was no space in my life for a relationship. I was busy evangelizing and advancing the Kingdom of God. I was completely sold out to the vision and purpose of the church; I was in love. I had found the Lover of My Soul. I had my Man, and there was no need for anyone else. My life was speaking and giving off a clear message. "If you're not Jesus or close to being Him, I'm not interested. I don't even see you!" Ha!

The Early Years

Believe it or not, my greatest desire when I was younger was to be married. When I think about that, it still makes me laugh! It's true. I wanted to be a wife who would love her husband, and whose husband loved her back. If I had that, my life would be complete. Or so I thought.

When I think back to those times, it amazes me to think that was my greatest desire. I was raised in an environment where education was the focus. C's were frowned upon, and anything below that was completely unacceptable. I brought home mostly A's and B's throughout my years in school. I was on the honor roll and graduated eleventh in my high school class. I went to college, graduated in three and a half years with a 3.5 GPA. I had such great potential, but it didn't matter as much to me. I would have given it all up to love and be loved.

I would sit for hours and talk about marriage with my aunt Cookie. She would say to me, "Sheila, wait until you're 40 to get married." I was like 40!! Are you kidding me? All I knew was that my heart was full of passion and joy, just thinking about the boys I liked, and who liked me. I would

10

often pray and ask God to send me someone that would love me. I wanted the feeling of someone loving me exclusively that would see the value in me to pick me. I wanted that special place in his heart. I guess somewhere down the line, I didn't feel as special as I needed to feel.

When I was around seven years old, I remember looking at my mother and saying, "You don't love me." I asked her about this when I was older, and to my surprise, she said, "You used to say that all the time." That was impactful because I remembered only the one time. To be clear, my mother loved me (shhh.... don't tell my sisters. I think I'm her favorite!), but as a self-centered child, I wanted more attention, affection, and affirmation. I craved it.

I reasoned to myself that, "If I can't get the love I want, I'll give it to somebody else." And that's exactly what I began to do! If I noticed someone who seemed sad or was having a bad day in school, I would go out of my way to encourage them. I enjoyed making other people happy, by simply listening to their problems. I felt like I was making a difference in their life. I was fully present and available for each friendship and took great pride and care as being a trustworthy friend. I loved genuinely from my heart. I gave people unconditional love and acceptance without judgement.

Loving from a place of non-judgment made me an ideal candidate to become a counselor. I was empathetic, a great listener, and I had a heart to see people find value in themselves. It was no surprise that I earned a master's degree in Counselor Education and became licensed as a Professional Counselor. I excelled in Graduate school as I learned so much about an area, I was naturally gifted in. My professors would often comment on how excellent my counseling skills were, which made me feel I had made the right career choice.

As I continued in my studies, I began to recognize that I had unhealthy patterns in relationships. I could see that I had co-dependent tendencies where I enabled and rescued others. These were the things I prided myself in as a "ride or die chick." This part of me seemed to be embedded in my DNA, and no matter how much I would try to get away from it, I kept finding myself pulled back into it. Faulty thinking and misplaced loyalties were setting me up for a big fall.

Love, Happiness and The Leap

There was no doubt, God called me. There was mounting evidence building year after year, from the people whose lives had been impacted by the gifts of grace God had given me. I was honored. I felt special, appreciated, and adored by many. All the things I longed for as a young girl, only packaged differently. My heart was full of gratitude that God chose me and loved me. I never imagined that my life would have had that kind of impact.

Like the exquisite beauty of a rose, I was a woman in full BLOOM.

There came a time where I began to outgrow, where I had been for 20 years. My appetite was changing. I was hungry for a new level in ministry and life. Something inside me was longing for more. I could always sense when I was nearing a transition, and this time was no different. It was only a matter of time. I would be moving.

I wasn't sure how I would take the leap. I had established deep roots and built a strong reputation where I was. If I left, I would have to start all over again. As I struggled to wrap my mind around this change, one of my spiritual mentors challenged me. She said, "What are you waiting for? God didn't call you to be a one town lady. You were meant for more."

Finally, I got the courage to leave. I quit my job, depleted my savings, and moved to Atlanta, GA. I found an affordable, swanky studio apartment in the heart of the city, with tennis courts and a small movie theater in the complex. I felt like things were off to a good start. Within a week, I had secured a job in my field and joined a progressive megachurch where every Sunday, I felt like the pastor was speaking only to me. It was exactly what I wanted and everything I needed.

It took me a little while to get acclimated. I was in a much larger city, and everything took 2-3 times longer than it did in the place I left. I learned patience as I had to wait in traffic, in the stores, and on the phones for customer service. I mean, EVERYTHING was slower here. Despite that, I loved being in Atlanta. It was a beautiful city full of progressive-minded black people with big dreams and big goals. Daily, I was surrounded by new opportunities and endless possibilities. I started teaching classes at my church and taking advantage of the numerous business opportunities. I started developing new friendships. And then finally, after over 15 years, I began to date.

New Chapter Moves

Dating was new to me, as my life before had been consumed with the ministry. With my move to a new city, I had fewer responsibilities, and I had more space for a relationship. As much as I wanted to be in a committed relationship, I was scared. My last dating relationship was sixteen years ago when I was twenty-two years old. Chronologically, I was in my 30's, but I was much younger developmentally when it came to dating. I was naïve and felt extremely uncomfortable and vulnerable. I had lived by a strict moral code and did not allow myself to be in situations that "woke me up" as a woman. It was hard for me to accept that I was human. To get what I desired (to be married), I had to go down the road less traveled. A road that made me want to run because I felt vulnerable and flawed.

I only dated a couple of guys before I met my husband. When he and I met, it was love at first sight. He was everything I wanted. He was a pastor and leader, packaged perfectly and confident in his pursuit of me. After a three-hour-long conversation in the lobby of our church, he said to me, "I'm going to marry you." A flood of emotions swept over me, and I felt like I had found my love, and my love had found me. We didn't waste a lot of time. I believed that it shouldn't take years for a man to know if a woman he's dating is his wife. Although this logic may be correct, there still needed to be sufficient time to get to know each other and be appropriately vetted. Something we did not do.

The following week we signed up for the next round of pre-marital counseling. We finished classes three months later and were married, exactly 12 months from the day we met. I knew without a doubt, I was meant to be married. Marriage suited me well. Many people would say, "marriage looks good on you." I felt like I was where I belonged. Soon after the wedding, I realized that marriage was for grown folks and not for the faint of heart. It was WORK, and this ride or die chick rolled up her sleeves and said, "Bring it on!"

I worked and worked. I fought and then fought some more. I refused to give up. I made a vow, and I wasn't going to take it back. Yet how do you handle something that seemed destined to fall apart? It was a hard place. On our first-year anniversary, one of my friends asked me, "Are you happy?" It saddened me that she noticed. I said, "No. Not at all." I could see the sadness in her eyes, yet I was determined to make the best of things. My friends began to worry. My BLOOM was starting to wilt.

Hard Lessons

"Get out of the way and let Me do in him what only I can do." I heard God say when I prayed about my marriage. Am I in the way God? Aren't I supposed to be a helper? My unhealthy relationship patterns were resurfacing as I tried to control things. I was afraid to let go. What will happen to our marriage? Will we grow apart? The fear of losing the thing I wanted most drove me to work even harder, trying to keep things from falling apart. I kept pushing, pleading, hoping,

14

and praying. It became too much. Five years into our marriage, we were divorced.

It was surreal. I had such a strange mix of emotions: relief, deep sadness, joy, and disappointment. I also felt a great sense of shame and embarrassment. How could we not make it work? We are leaders in the Body of Christ. I felt like I let so many people down. All those who held me in such high regard. What would they think? How would they see me now? I'm sure some judged, but I never knew. There was such an outpouring of love and compassion that surrounded me. My close friends and family shared that they had been praying for me. They seemed to let out a sigh of relief as they literally thanked God. That's when I knew. They understood. Even from afar, I'd lost the essence of who I was.

Although I was eager to get back to myself, the pain and confusion I felt demanded I take time to heal and grieve. The misplaced loyalties and faulty beliefs I had about what it meant to be a wife caused me to put aside many of the important things to me and perhaps even to God. Like Esau, I felt like I had traded my birthright for a pot of porridge. I was heartbroken as I believed that I let God down by devaluing and not honoring who He made me to be. I had voluntarily relinquished and downplayed the gifts of grace He had given me. I thought I was doing the right thing to dim my light. I wanted him to feel better about himself. Nobody asked me to do that! It was a result of my faulty thinking and misplaced loyalties.

I was blessed to have several therapists and friends who supported me as I worked through my grief. To help me move forward in a healthy way I conducted an "autopsy" of the marriage. I wrote out all the frustrations and problems I had with the relationship and my partner's issues. I looked at the choices I made and the results I got. I examined the pain I still felt and explored where I might have played a part in it. It was important to me that I face the truth and take ownership of my role in the marriage's demise.

The journey back to me took about three years. It was a lot longer than I imagined it would be. I came away understanding that not every person that comes into your life was meant to stay. Sometimes those relationships teach us lessons that enrich us and make us ready for God's ultimate plan. I learned not to take for granted the call of God on my life. To embrace it and never diminish it for anyone or any reason. I learned to allow the grace of God to transform me and reject the oppressive notion of perfection. I learned to appreciate and value who I am, knowing that I am a gift from God created for His glory. These are lessons I learned and what I pass on to the next generation.

Today, I celebrate Sheila Denise Reynolds. I honor her and the sacrifices she has made. I honor her courage, her passions, her flaws, her failures. I celebrate her journey and evolution as a grown, accomplished woman, I do this without apology and declare that her best is still yet to come.

Like the exquisite beauty of a rose, I AM a woman in full BLOOM.

LETHIA OWENS

A Zowie Yellow Flame represents endurance, daily remembrance, goodness and lasting affection.

This flower so powerfully represents transformation because of its unique gradient bicolor pattern. The Zowie Yellow Flame reminds us of our strength and capacity to endure the unimaginable and emerge more beautiful than ever.

Chapter 2

The Beauty of Transformation
Lethia C. Owens

One early morning in the cool fresh September air, I stood inside my bathroom mirror, asking myself one question, "Who am I?"

Sure, I could see my reflection in the mirror, but I couldn't really SEE my authentic self. When I looked past who others saw, thought, or whom they perceived me to be. I couldn't figure out who the woman was staring back at me.

The truth is, in this chilling moment, standing all alone in the complete silence of my bathroom. Without any distractions from the world, for the first time in a long time, I began to *really see* myself. I didn't like what I saw in the mirror.

It wasn't that I didn't love myself. It wasn't that I lacked confidence or had a poor self-image. I could see so clearly my sinful nature. It turned my stomach and brought me to my knees as I began to cry out. I asked God to help me become the woman. He created me to be.

You see, I was living a very busy and successful life. I knew God and loved Him. I had unknowingly adopted a performance-based mindset related to my relationship with God.

I was so busy doing the work of my heavenly Father that I was beginning to squeeze an intimate relationship with Him out of my schedule. I became so focused on **doing** for God that I began to overlook **being** with Him.

This doesn't work in any relationship, especially in my relationship with God. I believe the people who love us most want to be *with* us more than they want what we *do* for them.

Too often, our worth, identity, validation, and affirmation is wrapped up in what we do and how well we do it. I was caught up in the trap of thinking that God's love for me was based on what I did for Him and how well I did it.

When I was just a freshman in high school, I became a teen mom and had to drop out. My homeroom teacher Mr. Wilder told me that I would never amount to anything. I would most likely end up either on drugs or selling drugs. This experience taught me that I had to fight to show people that I was good enough.

I learned that when I work hard, I am rewarded. I earned a full-ride scholarship to attend college. I graduated top of my class, secured a prestigious job after graduation, and launched several successful businesses. I have been awarded an honorary doctorate in divinity. When you work hard, people will like you, and doors will open.

There is nothing wrong with being rewarded for hard work. However, when the primary motivation behind the hard work is to gain the respect, love, adoration, and approval of others, and not God, it can become a problem. Behind all of my rewards and success was a sinful secret. I wasn't working hard and accomplishing great things because I loved God. I was doing them **to be** loved by Him.

This morning in September was the beginning of one of my most powerful transformations. I had felt so far away from God, and I realized that it wasn't He who had left me. I had chosen to travel a path filled with selfish ambitions and the desire to earn the approval of men. On this day, I decided that I wanted the life God wanted for me. It became apparent that the life and success I deeply desired was on the other side of my YES to God.

Getting to the other side required me to go to a new level in my faith walk. I had to find the courage to let go of my rigid focus on spiritual disciplines as a measure of my faithfulness and worth to God, and let God transform me.

Transformation isn't easy, and it is often messy. But it is necessary. Think of the transformation of birth, your belly and body become unrecognizable. Your back hurt, your feet hurt, heck everything hurts. The actual birth is bloody, painful, exhausting, frightening, overwhelming, BUT necessary. Necessary in order to experience the beauty of the precious baby that follows the birth.

In Romans 12:1-2, Paul wrote to believers:

"I appeal to you therefore, brothers, by the mercies of God, to present your bodies as a living sacrifice, holy and acceptable to God, which is your spiritual worship. ²Do not be conformed to this world, but be transformed by the renewal of your mind, that by testing you may discern what is the will of God, what is good and acceptable and perfect."

The Greek word for transformed is *metamorphoo*, which is the root word for the English word metamorphosis. Simply put, a metamorphosis is to change from one form into another.

Paul describes this change in 2 Corinthians 5:17:

"Therefore, if anyone is in Christ, he is a new creation. The old has passed away; behold, the new has come."

Transformation requires total surrender. We cannot experience the new life God has in store for us until we surrender our will to His will. This means being uncomfortable. I've come to a place in my life where I would rather spend the rest of my days uncomfortable yet within the will of God than to spend the rest of my days in comfort outside His will.

In nature, metamorphosis is used to describe the transformation from a caterpillar to a butterfly.

The concept of transformation is difficult for our human minds to grasp. When in the midst of change, it is difficult not to focus on the suffering that goes with the transformation. We don't know the outcome. God does. It is during this time we need to trust that God knows what He is doing and that *He has made everything beautiful in its time.* (Ecclesiastes 3:11).

The butterfly is a picture of new life in Christ. Its metamorphosis illustrates a believer's spiritual transformation. Imagine you're a caterpillar. As you crawl on your belly, your view of the world does not change much. The caterpillar can be likened to someone who looks to find his identity in the world. No matter how much he feeds on the world's beliefs, he is never satisfied.

It is when we put our hope in Jesus as our Lord and Savior, that we find our purpose. We begin the process of becoming new creatures.

The Bible tells us that to experience our best life on this side of heaven; we must first die to self. In Galatians 2:19-20, Paul shares, *"For through the law I died to the law so that I might live to God. I have been crucified with Christ. It is no longer I who live, but Christ who lives in me. And the life I now live in the flesh I live by faith in the Son of God, who loved me and gave himself for me."*

What does it mean to die to self?

Billy Graham wrote: "To die to self is to set aside what we want at this moment and focus instead on loving God with everything we've got and valuing others as highly as we value ourselves (Matthew 22:37-39). This moves us away from self-centeredness and closer to becoming openhearted followers of Christ who care deeply for others. It's much easier to pay attention to the concerns, interests, and needs of people (Philippians 2:3-4) when our own interests no longer consume us."

There will come a time during transformation when you no longer recognize yourself...when, you no longer look like who you were, but you are not yet who you will become. You may even think, "I just don't feel like myself."

Think of the caterpillar as it begins its metamorphosis. It spins a little silk pad and forms a chrysalis that hangs upside down and is supported on a tree branch. Within the caterpillar are both its original cells and imaginal cells. During metamorphosis, the new imaginal cells begin to multiply, and the old cells break down basically into a rich bag of fluid.

During our own personal transformation, our old selves will often be at war with our new and improved selves. Every time you decide to step up and be better, say, "Yes" to God or do something of great importance, opposition will show up. Don't get discouraged. Just know that it is part of the process, and the opposition will make you stronger.

I can imagine how scared the caterpillar must be when all of a sudden, its legs fall off during metamorphosis. "Oh no God, my legs fell off. Wait, I need my legs!" That is how we often respond during our own transformations. We want the end result, but we are not too excited about the process and the things we will lose or give up to become more like Him.

A caterpillar no longer recognizes itself in the middle of transformation because it is no longer a caterpillar but not yet a butterfly.

Don't let transformation scare you. It is a beautiful process with many blessings. I am not the woman I once was, and I am not yet the woman I will become.

I want to encourage you to surrender to the transformation God wants to do in you. The caterpillar would have never become a beautiful butterfly if it didn't surrender to the process of transformation.

My name is Lethia C. Owens, and I will continue to BLOOM wherever I am planted.

ERICA STRONG

The "Miss Huff Lantana" represents rigor.
It is appreciated because it is easy to grow and
thrive in most soil conditions.

I liken myself and my life to the "Miss Huff Lantana"
flower. It is a beautiful yellow flower with a deep
orange center that survives by hibernating
underground through the winter, then bursting back to
life as summer arrives each year. It grows under
extreme heat and protects itself under extreme cold. It
adapts to its surroundings and knows how to survive.

Hello, I am Miss Huff Lantana, and I will
continue to bloom wherever I am planted.

Chapter 3

Three Superpowers:
Think, Believe and Affirm.
One Result: Abundant Life
Erica Strong

When my husband met an R&B singer at work and decided life with her was much more appealing, he left one day and never came back. Yes, you read that right, my husband went to work for an assignment out of town. Two weeks later, he called to tell me he wasn't coming home. I was left with no choice in the matter. I was forced to face a horrible, public divorce.

Depression engulfed me like a toxic windstorm; I thought that my life was over. I thought I would never be happy again. I assumed that I must have somehow brought this on myself. I began to drown myself in constant negative self-talk. I could not get out of bed for several days straight. I read a book by Joyce Myers titled *"The Battlefield of the Mind."* In her book, there was one point that changed my life. It started me on the journey of winning the battle over my mind. The point she made was that "the battle is either won or lost in your mind first."

I understood this to mean that if I think I have lost, if I think I am defeated, then I am. All the torture I was feeling at this point was self-inflicted. When my husband walked out of our home and never came back, his contribution to my pain was over; his part was done. I began to rehearse the events of the day in my mind. I started to analyze his motives, blame him and myself. I was now the culprit of my pain. My constant depressive, victim- minded, negative thoughts became my torturer. I made myself the enemy without realizing it. The pain was beginning to come from the inside. I was looking for someone or something on the outside to pin it to.

Seven years later, after I had done the work to heal and open myself up to love again. I met and married a "man of God," a pastor. I thought that I was finally safe because he was a man that knew God. He lived by His standard, or so I assumed. Not even a year into the marriage, I was challenged with another even more horrible and public divorce. This "knight and shining armor" turned into a nightmare. After the charm wore off, all I could see and feel from him was evil. He began treating me like I was only there to show up on Sunday mornings like a good little First Lady, and that was it. It was news to me to discover evidence that he was living a double-life on the "down-low."

Here I was again, slammed in the storm of devastation. Negative thoughts began to yell at me so loudly that the only way I could shut them out was to speak louder over them. I started using my voice to speak to myself. I would literally stop my thoughts and interrupt that inner chatter within myself. I began repeating a mantra to help me quickly realign my thoughts. In those moments, I would say, "I am safe, all is well, and God loves me." This would instantly stop the spiraling thoughts, giving me enough time to readjust my thinking. This was a full-time job

Training the way that you think about something moment by moment completely determines the outcome of your story and your life. I quickly realized that this "right-thinking" was my ticket to sanity and healing. I began teaching myself how to write personal affirmations and that is when my life completely changed. Affirming yourself is the most powerful thing you can do for yourself. It is by your words that you are justified and condemned. Those words usually start in your mind. Justification or condemnation will always be your choice.

Changing your life will take more than just reciting words or a daily mantra. My life did not start to change until I became overwhelmed with a deep conviction of what I was saying; a conviction I could physically feel. When you believe so deeply the very things you think or say, it will manifest in your life.

The scary truth about this is that you can also deeply believe such negative things about yourself that negativity will manifest. So careful vigilance over what you believe is what it will take to make the very thing you believe work for you and not against you.

If you really want to monitor what you believe, pay attention to a few clues. First, take a survey of the important things in your life. How do they look? How do they make you feel? Generally, our lives and our present situation is a direct product of what we believe. Example: You do not feel the level of success you thought you would feel at this stage in your life. Usually, the core antagonist in this dilemma is a subconscious belief that you are not qualified for the level of success you desire. This conflict of working hard to achieve success and doubting it would ever happen for you is the very thing holding it away from you. Would you believe that your success has more to do with what goes on inside you than any amount of work you put into it?

Second, acknowledge how you feel as often as you can throughout the day. Your emotions work as an alarm to remind you of what you believe. Example: You are driving your car while deep in thought. Suddenly you feel a sense of anxiety, stress, or worry. Now nothing has just happened, but you suddenly feel sad or depressed. In those moments, stop your thoughts. Ask yourself out loud, "What was I just thinking?" Most often, what just happened was your mind took you to a place of lack, scarcity, or fear of a particular situation, and your body immediately responded with an emotion.

Your emotional alarm is screaming, "WAIT...WAIT, what are you believing?" The only sign that tells what you believe is the reaction of your emotions. That emotional alarm is giving you the indication that something is wrong with what you are believing and an opportunity to correct it. If a sad or fearful thought comes up, and you quickly remind yourself out loud, "I believe I am favored, I believe I am enough, and I believe God loves me." You immediately allow what you believe to take over that moment. In an instant, you would feel ease, calm, and confidence, because of the circumstance, what you believe will always override it.

It is unfortunate, so many have become discouraged and mislead by the "name it and claim it" syndrome that has been taught for years in church causing one to believe all they need to do is just say it—say what you want, and it will magically happen. Let's take a moment to bring just a little more clarity to this concept. Your words are extremely valuable. We know life and death are in the power of your tongue; so, your words carry a lot of weight. You do not become what you say; you become what you believe. It is the powerful trio of your thoughts, your words, and your feeling or belief that will create your reality. Remember, whatever a man thinks in his heart, so is he.

This raises a question: how can a man think in his heart? Should that not say, "Whatever a man thinks in his mind?" It did not indicate mind, but specifically said in his heart. That means the heart is a pretty important point. The heart is where the truth is felt, where the trigger of emotion stems. So, what you think (believe, feel) in your heart, so you will become.

I truly believe Christ was able to perform so many miracles and do the unbelievable, not because He prayed all day, or because He knew God's Word, or because God spoke to him. He was able to do the unimaginable, the impossible because He believed He was the Word, He believed He was the beloved of God, He believed who He was in God. It was the confidence of His belief that produced His power, and that is

30

the same power you have. Jesus said, "Great things have I done, but even greater will you do." The example for greatness has been set. Now it is time to follow the path. *What do you believe?*

When you can merge the belief in your heart with the confidence in your mind (a heart and mind merger), you will be able to speak anything and see it happen for real. This means your heart has to be bursting with the truth of who you are—who you believe you are—and then continually relaying the message to your mind until the only words that come out of your mouth are words that beam from your place of truth, your foundation of belief, your inflamed feelings of confidence, your power source...your HEART! This is the power of belief. Whatever you think (believe) in your heart, you will become!

Let me share a glimpse of how I made all of this make sense to me, in an article written for "The Christian View" magazine:

Oneness in the Midst of the Storm Sitting in the middle of what seemed like hell, trying to think my troubles away and understand what was happening, with my senses firing on all cylinders, I could only see despair, feel hopelessness and hear my inner voice screaming, "there is no coming back from this." How could my life be in such turmoil and how do I find my faith in such a dark mess?

I was facing a divorce, displacement, financial calamity and an emotional breakdown all at one time. One day in the midst of my deepest depression as I regurgitated thoughts of everything that was going wrong in my life, I got out of the bed and headed for the shower. The shower was my hiding place to secretly cry without alarming my children and having them to worry about me and our next steps to stability. As their mother, I am supposed to have all the answers, right?!

I found relief and the answer to my despair in the most unlikely place. In the shower as I let out my wail and cried my heart out. I heard so clearly in my mind and felt so passionately in my heart; "I will Bless the Lord at all times, His praise shall continually be in my mouth" (Psalm 34:1). That scripture was so pronounced and so clear that I stopped crying almost immediately as if someone had just come in and caught me crying, I began repeating it out loud over and over until I felt a joy that surprised me. Why was I feeling this joy? My problems were the same, nothing had changed.

I didn't want to lose this feeling so I immediately got out of the shower and went to my Bible to read that scripture in full to gain more understanding. When I opened it, it opened to Mathew 6:33, "But, seek first the Kingdom of God and His Righteousness and all these things will be added to you." Right then, I felt the light bulb in my head beam bright, I got it! I finally understood what was happening. Are you ready for this? What I am about to tell you goes for any difficulties, any troubles, any turmoil in your life and gives you a solid Faith foundation. In the midst of any storm this is what you use to come out of it.

I began to understand "I will Bless the Lord at all times," meant never ceasing, always blessing the Lord through remembering the truth of who God is "at all times" good times, bad times, uncertain times, happy times. "His praise shall continually be in my mouth." Instead of believing what is happening around you, keep your mind and your mouth on what is true.

Right in the face of adversity, you say, God is with me. God is Love. God is in me. God is all that is Good, whatever you know about God to be only true. There is a reason that those two phrases stood alone, bless the Lord at all times. How? With continual praise, never stopping. Then I wondered why I went straight to Mathews 6:33? That scripture starts with "But," and we know that anything that starts with "But", just cancelled out whatever was before it. So when this scripture starts; "But, seek first the Kingdom of God and His Righteousness," I see that it is telling me that even though trouble has presented itself... "BUT, seek first," cancelling out the fear of that trouble because your faith is in "seeking first." This is the answer. When you seek the Kingdom of God first, it means that you are seeking your oneness with God, you are seeking your constant connection to God and you are declaring the truth of who God is and your unlimited power in Him. Saying, I and my Father are one. I am one with God and His Grace is upon me. There is no separation between my father and me.

When you cancel out the thoughts of any threats and replace them with your oneness with the Father, you are seeking His Kingdom and all of His Righteousness, this how you Bless the Lord and how His praise is constantly in your mouth. You will then see "All these things shall be added unto you." What things?? All health, grace, love, power, prosperity, wisdom, peace and all that God is. All these things are your birthright and connecting to your oneness with God at all times is how you walk in this power no matter what's happening around you. I am living proof that it works and God's word is true.

Repeat After Me... "I am One with God and His Grace is upon me. I am One with God and His Grace is upon me. I am One with God and His Grace is upon me." Now Believe it and Know It!!!

As we learn the beauty and blessings in our blooming, we are not afraid of the condition of the soil or the temperature of our environment, that we have to grow in.

We are charged and empowered, emboldened even, in the trust that our Father will cause us to bloom in the most unlikely of conditions.

My name is Erica Strong, and I will continue to BLOOM wherever I am planted.

Meet Erica Strong

Erica Strong was born in Baltimore, Maryland and now lives in Atlanta, Georgia. She is a mother of 3 daughters, a published author, business owner, celebrity stylist, motivational speaker, and life coach.

With over 20 years of styling experience, Erica has been graced with multiple opportunities within her industry. She has served as Educator for major hair care system, worked as one of the lead stylists for Mercedes Benz New York Fashion week, styled for runway and print, as well as held the position as Head of Hair for feature films. She has worked with amazing producers/directors such as Kim Fields, Tyler Perry, Tommy Ford, and James Kicklighter.

Erica has traveled extensively sharing her message of hope and redemption her talent of styling and the reprogramming of the mind. This transformation in the mind will lead to a transformed life. She has a great passion for inspiring others and establishing the validity of their personal worth. Erica has dedicated the next phase of her career to helping others to advance to higher levels, both professionally and personally.

Her motto and the force that drives her is "Successful Minds = Successful Lives."

Website: www.ericastrong.com
Instagram: https://www.instagram.com/finishingstrong/
Facebook: https://www.facebook.com/ericastrongcoach

ANGEL ALLEN TOWNSEND

An Iris represents
hope, faith and courage.

I chose the Iris because I've had to employ all of
these traits to help me get through more than one
traumatic experience and they've served me well
again and again. The Iris looks elegantly beautiful,
fragile, strong and complex, all at the same time;
just like the tapestry that is my life.

Chapter 4

The Truth
Angel Allen Townsend

I was only fifteen when I met thirty-eight-year-old Chuck at the department store. I'd fibbed about my age to get the job. Things started innocently enough between us. He asked me about school and whether I liked my job working behind the candy counter.

My life at home was tumultuous, so I welcomed his compliments and small talk. He made me feel appreciated, and he seemed genuinely interested in the answers I gave to his probing questions. Before long, though, his seemingly harmless interest turned sinister. His conversation went from schoolwork and my job to whether I had a boyfriend and my appearance. Even though I'd seen and experienced a lot, I was still trusting and didn't think of people as evil predators.

At more than twice my age, with probably years of experience taking advantage of young girls, Chuck knew just what to say to make me believe he was harmless. One evening, he invited me over to 'talk.' I eagerly accepted, looking forward to getting away from the chaos my father kept going at home. I also needed a break from my cheating boyfriend and his verbally and emotionally abusive mother. I let my mom know that I was going to hang out with a friend. I lied when she asked me who this friend was, giving her the name of one of my girlfriends that she knew. This friend's sister brought me home often. She gave her permission, telling me that I had to be home before 11.

Chuck waited outside until I got off. When I got in his car, I felt that something was off. He was quiet and never looked at me. "Hey," he said, as he started the car and pulled out of the parking space.

"Hey!" I replied excitedly.

"Thanks for inviting me over. I can only stay a little while. I have to be home by eleven."

"Yeah, I'll have you home by then. We're just gonna hang out and talk.

"Cool. You ok? I asked. "You seem distracted."

"Nah, I'm good. Just had a busy day at work."

We rode the rest of the way in silence. When we got to his apartment, he unlocked the door, and we walked inside.

"So, do you want ice cream first? He asked. "Or do you want to have sex, then ice cream?"

I looked at him like I'd been punched in the face. "What?" He replied.

"I remember what you told me. I know how much you like ice cream, so I got you some. You know we're having sex tonight, right?

I was shocked and scared. I didn't know how I was going to get out of there.

"So, what, ice cream first?"

I didn't know what to do.

"Um…ice cream, I guess." The words surprised me as they left my mouth.

He prepared me a bowl of ice cream and began to get undressed. He watched me eat my ice cream. Tears rolled down my cheeks as I slowly ate my ice cream. I began to feel sick to my stomach. I felt as though there was no way I could escape this monster.

At one point, he said, "Hurry up! What's taking you so long?! I need to get you back home soon. I gotta go to work in the morning!"

When I finally finished my ice cream, he took the bowl and told me to go to the bedroom, get undressed, and get in bed. I felt scared, small, and helpless. I did exactly as I was

38

told. He came in, climbed on top of me, and he raped me, without one word between us. When he finished, he got up and told me to go clean myself up. During the drive to my house, I looked out the window and whimpered quietly, shocked by what had just happened.

He seemed almost giddy as he talked about how "sweet and juicy" I was and how he couldn't wait for us to get together again. I couldn't respond. I knew that my voice would break from painful emotion if I tried. When we got to my house, as I opened the door and moved to step out of the car, he said, "I'll call soon so we can get together again! That was your favorite ice cream, right?"

He squeezed my butt as I wordlessly stepped out of the car without so much as a glance back at him. He chuckled as I closed the door, pulling off before I'd taken two steps.

A preferred ending to this story would be that I reported the rape, that he was arrested, convicted, and imprisoned for violating me the way he did that night. That would have been justice, but that's not what happened. Instead, I went inside, hiding my tears and my shame. Fortunately, it was late, and everyone was in bed for a change. I took a two-hour bath, attempting to scrub the shame and pain away. I cried myself to sleep that night. In the morning, I pulled myself together, and I never told.

When Chuck walked up to the candy counter a few days later, he acted happy to see me and chatted like we were best friends. I don't know how it happened, but the scenario of that awful night repeated itself many times over the next several months.

My life was a whirlwind of trauma and abuse. My father was usually drunk and his verbal and emotional abuse seemed relentless. My mom was trying to juggle the multiple balls of work, running interference between her beloved children and the husband she wanted to love back to emotional health and sanity. She also ensured that we had a roof over our heads and food in our bellies. With all of this going on, she barely had time to notice that my life was spiraling out of control.

I bounced between Chuck and my "real" boyfriend L.T. L.T. flaunted his infidelity in my face. His mother, Mary, not only approved of it; she also made me feel like I deserved it. She regularly belittled me, while I tried in vain to please her. I began to feel as though I deserved to be cheated on. I felt unworthy of respect or healthy love.

I began to disrespect myself. The way I treated myself reflected the way I allowed others to treat me. I talked negatively to myself. I began to use drugs and alcohol. I thought I was having fun, but I was attempting to numb the excruciating pain. I learned to believe all the ugly lies I told myself. The biggest lies were that I wasn't good, pretty, or worthy enough to have good things happen in my life.

Paradoxically, it was during this time that my strong spiritual foundation was built. Both of my grandparents were active members of the church. My grandfather was a Deacon. He sat on the treasury board, and he helped build the church we called home for years. His name can still be seen on the church building's cornerstone on Rose and Harding in Rockford, IL.

The first bomb was dropped in our lives when my dad was sentenced to 25 to 40 years in a maximum-security prison after an argument with a coworker that went terribly wrong. My mom, grandfather, and I witnessed the event. Shortly after that, when I was only six years old, we moved across town into a house across the street from my maternal grandparents. It was a move that added much-needed stability to our lives. Our mom was able to keep working full time as a registered nurse while we were under the safe and watchful eyes of our grandparents.

Being in their care meant spending tons of time in church. We were in church four out of seven days every week! Service on Tuesday and Friday nights, choir rehearsal on Saturday and all-day Sunday, starting with Sunday school and ending with Sunday night service.

It felt like too much as we got older. We wanted to hang out with our friends from the neighborhood. We went to the church with good friends who were our age. Many of the adults made Sunday school and choir rehearsal fun. We learned about the love of God and the importance of faith and hope that could sustain us through troubling times. We ate together, sang, and traveled together. Even today, decades later, we maintain good relationships with the church friends of our youth.

Our beloved choir director, whom we all affectionately call Aunt Cle and her sweetheart of a sister, Aunt Lee, loved us and encouraged us. They also reprimanded us when they needed to. Along with several others, they provided an example of love, kindness, respect, accountability, and responsibility. Their consistent leadership supported a strong foundation of unwavering love, hope and faith, honesty, patience, integrity, teamwork, and inner strength. These are the qualities that our mother exemplified every day in our home.

Before my daddy went to prison and even during most of his lengthy incarceration, I was the epitome of a daddy's girl. I was, from the moment I emerged from my momma's womb, my daddy's little princess. I was, as were my sister and brother, when they came along later, the apple of both of my parent's eyes. They loved all three of us unconditionally. I'm sure they saw hope, joy, and the promise of a bright future in us. All of this is true, but being my parents' firstborn *and* a girl, I believe I held a special place in my daddy's heart. Don't we all, though? Blessed are the children whose parents make each of them feel special and especially loved, as ours did!

Knowing that my parents supremely loved me gave me confidence, joy, and peace. My mom and dad instilled the belief that I could succeed at whatever I put my mind to. They listened to me, encouraged me, and challenged me to think for myself; to figure things out, and to bloom!

When my daddy was suddenly snatched from my everyday life due to his incarceration, I was dealt a soul blow that shook me to my core. I realize now that I was traumatized by what I'd witnessed that day.

For a long while, I was withdrawn and depressed. When I was just starting to regain my emotional footing, my daddy was released. He brought misplaced, pent up rage, alcoholism, and abuse into the peaceful sanctuary that our mom had created for us. This disruption led to years of dysfunction. I abused alcohol and drugs and became involved in abusive relationships with men who claimed they "loved" me.

What I know now is that many people face what I've faced with much more devastating outcomes. What I know is that I'm not "special" but had certain interrupters that became my lifelines.

What did I do to step onto a path to better health and peace? How did I uncover the truth of who I am - God's beloved daughter (Ephesians 5:1), Jesus' baby sister (Galatians 4:4-6; Romans 8:17), in Whom I am more than a conqueror (Romans 8:37)?

I wasn't aware that the early foundation of faith and hope (Hebrews 11:1) laid by my mom, grandfather, and church family helped sustain me through it all.

If not for the strong foundation that was a part of my DNA, I could have easily been a statistic instead of sharing my healing and redemption story with you. Whether this foundation was laid early for you or not by parents or others, don't be mistaken; God has planted this seed in each of us. (Romans 5:5) Your innate desire for more, for better, for different, is clear evidence that God is calling you forward. This anthology finding its way into your hands isn't a coincidence! Believe the call is for you and answer it!

These seeds of faith and hope planted in me provided an inner strength that caused me to find ways to keep fighting when I was emotionally and mentally exhausted.

There were times when I was too beat down, too depressed, or too high to feel hopeful. When I couldn't pray or speak life over myself, I had a team of cheerleaders and faith-walkers who stood in the gap. My mom and siblings, Debra and Dean were there. Two special aunts, Elois and Candy, and at different times, one friend or another, prayed for or with me, admonished me and reminded me of my greatness, my options, and theirs and God's love for me.

Support is paramount to my success! I lovingly suggest that you identify those you want to be your cheerleaders, prayer partners, and voices of honest reason if you don't have a team now. We're all stronger together. Ecclesiastes 4:12 says, *"Though one may be overpowered, two can defend themselves. A cord of three strands is not quickly or easily broken."* Develop or strengthen those relationships now, so that when challenging times arise, your crew is already in place.

My inquisitive mind that both my parents nurtured early on, served me well. To quote one of our powerhouse ancestors, Fannie Lou Hamer, when I eventually got "sick and tired of being sick and tired," I began to educate myself on the power of this beautiful mind God has blessed each of us with. I had to accept that ignorance of the truth is no excuse, and that I must get serious about putting my powerful thoughts to work for me instead of against me. Proverbs 23:7 states, *"as we think in our hearts, we are."*

I learned that what I focus on is a decision. Sometimes, when we've been hurt, we want to hold onto the anger. I know I did for far too long! I wanted lightning to strike Chuck and my other abusers! I'd pray, "Git 'em, God! Make him feel the pain I felt!" But, as I studied the mind, I came to understand that we draw to us what we focus on (Romans 12:2; Proverbs 26:27). I was reminded of a rhyme we used to say as kids: "I'm rubber and you're glue! Everything you plan for me, bounces off me and sticks to you!"

With conscious and considerable effort, I began to shift my thoughts to what I wanted my life to look like; a life filled

43

with joy and peace. Slowly at first, but eventually, I found that my blinding anger was melting away with increasing consistency. I'm not saying that I wanted to find these guys and hang out with them, but when they crossed my mind, I didn't feel sick to my stomach or the overwhelming sadness and shame I'd felt for so long.

My dad eventually chose sobriety and committed his life to God. He asked for forgiveness. He listened when I expressed the pain and heartache I experienced because of his brokenness. Our relationship began to heal when I decided to hold him in light and love (Numbers 6:24-26) every time I thought of him. Thinking alone may not make it so, but change cannot begin until thoughts change.

Please pay attention to what you think about yourself, your world, your circumstances, your options, and your future! Spend time consciously training your mind to be and stay positive. I promise the results will be worth your effort.

There is so much beauty in nature! Nature exemplifies the infinite creativity and boundless abundance of God. I have always been drawn to the Iris. Its brilliant colors and intricate beauty intrigue me. When I learned that the Iris symbolizes faith, hope, wisdom, and courage, among other characteristics, my affinity with this striking flower deepened.

Some of the soul blows that living this life delivers require courage to face and overcome. Some blows will require courage to tell! Some blows will require courage to seek help to face and deal with. For many years I was ashamed of what had happened to me, of what I experienced. Our society has a way of making those who experience sexual, physical, or other abuse forms feel like it's their fault. IT IS NOT!

Bullies and predators are cowards. They run for cover when light is shown on their dirty deeds. Ignore their lies or the voice in your head that keeps you captive. You deserve to be free and freedom requires courage. Having faith and hope in God's plans for your life can help give you the courage to keep going and strive for the life of your dreams. Lean on God's word and remember to ask for the wisdom promised to each of us in James 1:5.

Today, I finally believe the Truth. The Truth is that I am wonderfully made (Psalm 139:14); that although weapons *will* be formed against me (Isaiah 54:17), they won't prosper when I think (Proverbs 23:7) and decree rightly so good things will be established in my life. (Job 22:28) I still consciously work on maintaining a healthy outlook on life. I continue to speak life over myself and my circumstances. I strive for a close relationship with God, and I ask for wisdom daily. I surround myself with healthy friends, and we support each other in being our best selves.

I hope that my story will inspire you to recognize the Truth of your inner beauty and strength. I hope that you will be encouraged to nurture and water the garden of your soul, so that (John 6:63) all the brilliance that lives inside you BLOOMS magnificently!!

My name is Angel Allen Townsend, and I will continue to BLOOM wherever I am planted.

Meet Angel Allen Townsend

Angel is a graduate of Illinois State University with a bachelor's degree in Communications. She is an Author, Speaker and Certified Life Coach who is passionate about teaching others how to change their life by changing their thinking. Angel has received extensive training in mindfulness and guided meditation. Her work has successfully assisted clients to break unhealthy habits, accept themselves and live more peaceably.

"Family first" is Angel's motto. She takes great pride and joy in being a caretaker for her mom, as well as being a loving wife and big sister to her siblings. Angel's faith in God has been a powerful anchor through many tumultuous seasons of her life.

Facebook: https://www.facebook.com/goodlifeangel
Instagram: https://www.instagram.com/goodlifeangel1/

AUDREY DEBARROS

An Easter Lily represents purity,
hope and new life of Spring.

The Easter Lilly is one of my favorite flowers and
Rumi's quote sums up the meaning of this flower
perfectly. "The rose does best as a rose. Lilies make the
best lilies. And look! You - the best you around!"

During the Easter season, I would buy an Easter Lily
and after the flowers dropped off, I would plant it in
the back yard and wait for it to bloom again in Spring.
This plant helps me to remember when in
relationships, I am given an opportunity for spiritual
growth and to remember the true essence I am (Love).

Chapter 5

My Journey to Discovering Self-Love
Audrey DeBarros

My life's purpose is to be the best extension of God as a messenger for love. I am well poised to bloom in ways I could never have imagined I would bloom in this incredible season of life. Life is such a remarkable teacher. It is designed perfectly to allow us to become our authentic selves. I am so grateful for the lessons I have learned and continue to learn. No matter the appearance or shape, these lessons may take. I don't regret any of my experiences because I would not bloom and become who I am meant to be without them.

Relationships are powerful gifts that have supported my personal, emotional, and spiritual growth. This chapter will disclose relationships in my life that I now am aware that were perfectly designed for my awakening to self-love. While these significant gifts were not necessarily packaged with special wrapping paper or colorful bows, they were, nonetheless, gifts.

My parents were my first gift in my relationship growth experience. They brought me into the world as their second child. We grew into a family of eight (five girls and one boy).

I knew I was loved, even though I did not always feel love how I wanted it. We were blessed with wonderful parents that ensured each of us was cared for. We had a roof over our heads; we were clothed and fed. These necessities are truly the way a child knows they are loved. Why did I feel so alone? Why did I need to feel loved more emotionally? We were not the kind of family who talked about our feelings. We never discussed painful emotions or shared our hopes and dreams. We just followed the program set out for us.

My mother did a superb job modeling the domestic formula. I discovered if I followed her model, I could get the love I so desired. So, I cleaned the way my mother liked us to clean. I helped her with my baby brother. I learned the role of a wife/mother. I became a people pleaser. The missing part of the formula was modeling on how to express my emotions in a healthy way. I wanted to feel heard, loved, and understood.

There were times I felt like a fly on the wall. I would see the unhealthy ways my parents communicated with each other. As children, we never see the complete picture of our parent's relationship. We were not privy to how they communicated behind closed doors. Unintentionally, I would overhear hurtful comments by my dad and quiet acceptance by my mother.

I remember they argued one night. The next day, my mother prepared my dad's breakfast and packed his lunch. In return, my father gave my mother a non-affectionate half kiss goodbye. Where was the genuine affection?

As time passed, I observed more unhealthy emotional interactions between my parents. From that moment on, I decided I would never allow anyone to treat me that way. My cycle of feeling powerless continued. The lesson to learn was, it is okay to use my voice to speak my truth and stand up for myself. Life would give me many more opportunities to learn this lesson.

Fast forward to the evolution of my current chapter. My life journey has brought me into a heightened awareness. I can appreciate now that I am more loved, powerful, intelligent, loving, talented than my old self had been willing to accept. I was beginning to learn more about who I am and who I am meant to be, this spiritual being having a human experience.

The spiritual journey I had embarked on over the past thirty years helped me navigate this human terrain of life. I would often either flow with ease or feel as if I was rolling an enormous rock uphill. The most impactful lessons on my path to self-love were learned through romantic relationships. I realize these intimate relationships were mirror reflections of the relationship I had with myself. This self-awareness represented the hidden part of myself that needed either embracing or healing.

An Opportunity for Self-love

After twenty years, I thought I would have married again. At least, in 2-5 years after divorcing my first husband. When I married my second husband, I was ready for marriage. I grew tired of carrying the burdens of life on my own. I was under the impression that the old wounds from the first marriage had been healed. I assumed I had learned the necessary lessons to move on and start a fulfilling relationship.

During the intervening years, I found myself attracting men that were either emotionally or physically unavailable. What was getting in the way of finding my true love? In my search to find the perfect man, I prayed for help. I created a vision board and made a list of what I was looking for in a husband. I began to experiment with dating sites.

My life significantly changed during the summer of 2007. I sold my home of nineteen years in Roswell, GA. I was unsure of where I would plant myself to start a new chapter. I accepted an offer from my cousin and his wife to live at their place. My cousin felt indebted to me after living with me for years before meeting his wife.

In three months of dating online with eHarmony, I met the man of my dreams. Well, not exactly! He was nothing like the men I had dated. He came to me in a different package. He looked exceptional on paper...a Psychologist with two PhDs, and he owned a beautiful home located in Marietta, GA. He drove a Mercedes, he was single, and we shared spiritual beliefs. While I was not attracted to him right away, I decided to give him a chance.

Given my track record with men was not good, I figured God was running the show this time. Michael exhibited many characteristics on my list. A few of his attributes were not to my preference.

I assumed that I could accept his flaws, and things would improve over time. Without much delay, we married on January 1, 2008, after only two months of living together. We were both in our late fifties, entering our second marriage after twenty years. In retrospect, it was an irrational justification!

As we evolved in our relationship, I found myself more attracted to his intelligence than the physical chemistry. While we had similarities in our spiritual pursuits., our cultural differences influenced how we related to one another. He was born in Memphis, TN. He was given to his father's mother to be raised, separate from his other siblings and biological mother. I was raised with five siblings in a two-parent household by Cape Verdean parents in Springfield, MA. We were one of those relationships where opposites attract.

The way Michael's mind worked amazed me. His natural gifts were intriguing. I was insecure about what Audrey brought to the relationship. I would watch and listen to him in awe as he would masterfully use his unique gifts to persuade others to think beyond their self-imposed limitations. This was Michael's way of operating whether he was selling a house, making an informed purchase, or confronting me about what he considered unacceptable behavior.

Michael lived life on his terms, whether others approved or not. He exposed me to some of the finer things in life. His philosophy was adopted from an Oscar Wilde quote; "I have the simplest of taste, the best of everything will do." Michael enjoyed fine dining, brand labels, like Armani or Escada, and going on a Transatlantic cruise for sixteen days.

While this lifestyle was not as important to me, I enjoyed our adventures, and I was grateful for the exposure.

We often bumped heads in our communication style. It was as if he was trying to mold me into someone I wasn't. He wanted me to live life the way he did. It was the way Michael would speak to me when we disagreed that offended me. I could not live up to his standards. The sadness, hurt, and judgment I felt, off and on, implanted a sense of feeling powerless and helpless in me during our marriage. His huge all-consuming personality and energy increased my feelings of inadequacy. I often felt exposed and vulnerable. There was a lingering old familiar limiting belief, "I am not enough," echoing in my ear. There were times I would shut down for two-three days, and my husband would say, "my wife is like Jesus. It takes her three days."

Over time, I began losing my voice. I unintentionally gave up my power, acquiescing to him. I wasn't aware of how to fight in a healthy way. In my mind, he was playing a dual role; husband and psychologist. I felt more like I was his patient, instead of his wife. My son told me years later that I was becoming a fraction of myself in that relationship. The way I responded to conflict was a fight or flight response. So, to avoid conflict, I found myself rehearsing how to raise an issue with him while protecting my feelings.

Over the years, I attempted to understand him. Why was he so harsh? Why did he feel the need to be so controlling? I built up the compassion for his abandonment issues and being a recovering alcoholic. Yet, where was his compassion and understanding for me? Where was my soft place to land in our relationship?

During the first four years into the marriage, I knew I was unhappy. I decided to stick it out. I wanted to make my marriage work, especially because of my past failure.

The impact Michael began to have on me started to leave an indelible mark on my psyche. This issue prompted me to spend more time working on myself, spiritually, and emotionally.

The Unresolved Pattern

Reflecting on my first marriage, I hoped old wounds had healed. I soon realized that I had only placed a band-aid on old wounds. My limiting beliefs and low self-esteem had carried over into my second marriage.

In my first marriage, I desired a certain level of attention from my husband. I convinced myself that he was not behaving the way a husband "should" behave. I would lay in our marital bed, wondering where he was at night. Thoughts of him being in an accident would cross my mind. My first husband was seven years older than me. His dreams were not my dreams. He wanted to buy a house. I wanted to travel or engage in more social events. I wanted children. He already had two children and didn't want more.

In the first year of marriage, I conveniently neglected my birth control pills. I soon became pregnant with our son.

The unconditional love I had for my son seemed to fulfill the love I was craving from my husband. At least, while I attempted to figure out our marriage. Self-love was something I was unfamiliar with at the time. I was looking for love to come from other people. The love and attention I desired seemed to elude me. My insecurities led me to believe my husband was the problem. Not me.

I got married at twenty-five. I finished college and began working in my career field. I struggled with communicating my emotions and expressing what I needed in my marriage. I set expectations for my husband, selfishly, without having a clear vision for our marriage. My mindset was coming from the default program in my upbringing. I'd adopted the recurring pattern of my voice, not mattering. I struggled with expressing my feelings because I was not heard. I learned to suppress and stifle myself. I interpreted this behavior as being a people pleaser. My emotional immaturity became more evident throughout my marriage. I expected my husband to understand my feelings without me having to tell him.

After our son was born, my husband went on a 6-week Air National Guard assignment, and I did not know how to handle him being away that long. As I dropped him off at the airport, my immature emotional self-gave meaning to this temporary separation as rejection. I found myself attracted to someone other than my husband. Someone who would give me the love and attention I desired. I felt ashamed of my actions and confessed my sins when my husband returned.

My parents came to my rescue when my husband reacted violently toward me during an altercation. I lived with my parents until I was able to get back on my feet. After the divorce, I decided to go to counseling. I had the mistaken belief that I was supposed to figure out my problems on my own. However, as part of a support system, incredible sister-friends offered a safe space for me to feel heard, comforted, and loved.

This experience revealed to me that I had bought into societal programming for the path in my life. I had not yet figured out the vision for my life.

Examining Unresolved Patterns

My second marriage exposed my emotional triggers. I ignored them. In hindsight, these were the same insecurities and esteem issues of the past. I came to the understanding that I was repeating the learned behavior I adopted from my mother.

As I reflect on the past thirteen years, I am mesmerized by what it took for me to accept my life. Genesis 1:26 asserts that humankind is made in "the image of God." The truth is, it took what it took, and I am truly grateful to still be on my journey. The lessons I discovered through my experiences awakened me to realize who I am. God did not create other than Himself and I am grateful for the lessons.

The Healing Begins

Therefore, if anyone is in Christ, he is a new creation. The old has passed away; behold, the new has come, 2 Corinthians 5:17. It was time for me to start the healing process and take my spiritual studies and practices to another level. It was time to remove the blocks that only, with the help of the Holy Spirit, could unlock the blocks to Self-love.

Resources and teaching tools were made available to me when I was ready for them. The work I did with Colin Tipping's Radical Forgiveness program offered a transformative approach that helped me begin to discover peace, love, and acceptance of myself. Also, I continued to affirm Lesson 34 in A Course in Miracles, "Forgiveness is my only function as the light of the world." Also, I attended Alon-on meetings, even though Michael was no longer drinking. These sessions were empowering and assisted me to respond differently to the challenges I would go through. I had been allowing dysfunctional thought patterns of fear to keep me prisoner, and I was ready to surrender all.

Early in 2013, during a moment of need, I was prompted to reach out to Rev. Barbara, my teacher, friend, confidant, and spiritual sister, to request that we resume our weekly studies. The timing could not have been more perfect because she was being called by God to resume her private classes but differently than before. She was being called to formulate and conduct Spiritual Therapy sessions.

My prayers for guidance were answered. As we joined with the Holy Spirit in our sessions, I felt supported to take responsibility for challenges in my marriage and wake up to my true divinity.

I was on my journey to Self-love. I was ready to surrender and release the insecurities, comparing myself to others, self-judgment and my fears, to the One Presence and One Power God the Good Omnipotent. I was blessed with the will

56

to choose, so; it is time for me to choose love without conditions.

When I wanted to make myself wrong, criticize, or judge rather than learn, grow, and evolve, life was difficult instead of fulfilling. Love begins within. Love requires remembering who I am and reclaim the truth of my being. "and you will know the truth, and the truth will set you free," John 8:32.

The moment arrived in 2016; I could no longer live the way I was living with my husband. I was losing Audrey; I was not happy; something was shifting in me; my emotional well-being was at stake. My husband unknowingly gave me the way out. In this defining moment, it was as if I was watching myself in a movie, floating through the drama to safety. If I did not choose to leave when the opportunity presented itself, my light would have dimmed even more. I realized I must reclaim who God created me to be, not remain as this insecure, people pleaser I thought I needed to be loved.

I am with you to deliver you. Jeremiah 1:8

In my first step walking out the door, leaving the comfort zone and shelter we had created, was the beginning of loving myself enough to take a risk and put Audrey's needs first. Letting go was a stressful process while walking into the unknown as I moved forward. I was feeling too fragile, broken, and emotionally raw to continue in my marriage. To maintain sanity and ensure self-care, it was important for me to be gentle with myself and avoid judging myself or Michael. This transition period was a whirlwind experience.

God sent incredible sister-friends into my life. Some from my past and others that would be part of my future walk. They rallied around me with unconditional love, compassion, prayer, and unwavering support. These women joined me in dedicating our thoughts in union with God. I was so grateful for divine right action in my life and affairs during this journey as I embraced Self-Love. Every step I took was with God's grace and in divine order.

Divorcing Michael was liberating yet sad because shortly after the divorce was final, he made his transition. Since he has passed on, I feel his loving presence more now than when we were married. His son and I worked together to create a memorable home-going that Michael would have been pleased to see he was loved, even though he did not always make it easy to love him.

Divine intervention is my saving grace. God blessed me with the courage to be me and the willingness to surrender what was no longer serving my highest and best Self. Michael was the consummate life teacher for me, and I will be eternally grateful for who I am becoming because of the lessons he helped me to learn.

My journey now is Self-Love, compassion, understanding, acceptance and trust in the Divine Presence in me as me. I choose to be gentle, kind and nurturing with myself, living life through the grace of God, as a messenger of love. Awakening to my divine Self, is a freeing experience.

I embrace these new beginnings with wonder and surprise because, as my teacher Rev. Barbara has quoted to me, God is a God of wonder and surprise. I am now more than ever, open and receptive to the living Spirit of truth and to His instruction and guidance.

My prayer for future generations is for you to be willing to deepen your connection to a power greater than yourself. No matter where you are and where your path takes you and who is with you, treasure the truth: you are an individualized extension of God!

Step into your greatness! Embrace opportunities to choose for love instead of fear. We are all powerful beyond measure. As we bloom, let us walk together as One.

My name is Audrey DeBarros, and I will continue to BLOOM wherever I am planted.

Meet Audrey DeBarros

Audrey DeBarros is President of DeBarros Ltd, a Human Resource Consulting, Training and Coaching business based in Henderson, Nevada, and the founder of Coaching for Greatness.

Audrey has a Master's degree in Human Technology along with life coaching certifications. She is a seasoned professional with an extensive background in Diversity and Inclusion, Executive Coaching, Management Development, and Organization Change Initiatives.

In her dedication to working collaboratively with others, Audrey is passionate about nurturing the growth and development of individuals and teams. Her intention is to deliver to those she services, experiences that allow for personal transformation. She is highly regarded as an inspiring coach, strong facilitator/trainer, and engaging college professor. She has a trustworthy style and ability to connect with diverse audiences to encourage, allow and inspire them to be their highest and best Self.

As her essentials in life, Audrey is committed to her spiritual evolution, spending time loving on her two beautiful grandchildren, engaging in fun excursions with family and friends, listening to uplifting music as well as embracing the growth opportunities that life presents on her path.

Favorite quote: "Each of us must be the change we want to see in the world." Gandhi 1930

BARBARA PATTERSON

*An Azalea represents temptation,
caution and danger.*

*The Azalea is my flower because it only comes in the
Spring for the most part. It stays around for a short
period of time and then it withers up and die. It is the
soft delicate petals and if you brush against it gently it
falls to ground. The Azalea has a distinct look from
beauty to ugliness. It is beautiful to look at in full
bloom but when its time is over, it is not very pretty to
look at. So was life during this pregnancy.*

Chapter 6

An Unexpected Life and Unexpected Blessing
Barbara Patterson

So many times, I thought I knew better than God. Only to discover, He always knows what's best for me. Like the Azalea, I was delicate and easily found myself falling to the ground. I endured painful circumstances that made me want to wither away. The spring of life was on its way with the beauty of the full bloom.

Early Years

I grew up in a two-parent household in Jacksonville, North Carolina. My father was a smart college-educated military man. Although he was witty and charming, he had two sides to his personality. For instance, whenever he would become upset with my mother, he would refuse to pay the bills. The responsibility to keep the family together fell on my siblings and me. We often had to fend for ourselves. Our mother was unable to work a lot due to epilepsy. She was rather sickly.

After graduating from high school, I wanted to get away from home, so I moved to Hawaii. I knew one thing for sure; I was never going to get married or have children. I had big plans of traveling the world and visiting exotic places. But as fate would have it, things did not turn out that way. I moved back home.

Marriage and My Mac

Marriage was not a part of the plan. I was supposed to be traveling the world! When I met my husband Mac, he got my attention. There was something different about him. He was three years younger and more mature than most men. He was a genuinely compassionate, caring, and empathic man. He protected and cared for me. Although I was fiercely independent, I needed someone to love and care for me. The pain of my childhood was unknowingly impacting me in ways I did not understand. Mac became a constant source of compassion and support.

After six years of dating, Mac's consistency and stability drew me in. I accepted his marriage proposal, even though I was uncertain. My uncertainty came from insecurities about being a good wife. I brought a lot of baggage into the marriage. I struggled to adjust to my new life. Things became worse when I became pregnant. Like the Azalea, I was getting ready to go through a season where I would wither up and feel like dying.

The Pregnancy

We were married five years when I became pregnant. At six weeks, I discovered that I was severely anemic and that my blood cells were not as healthy as they should have been. The doctor was surprised I was able to walk into his office. He told us that I did not have enough blood to share with the baby and that the baby or I may die during childbirth. If I decided to carry the baby to term, I would be on best rest the entire pregnancy. I would only be able to go out for a doctor's appointment and then back to bed.

To be told, I could no longer come and go as I pleased made me very upset and confused. I could not accept that I would not be working, traveling, or driving; I became even angrier when the doctor told us that he would not continue as my doctor and that he would help me find one in my area. I felt completely out of control.

My life turned upside down. I was in a state of shock. I had to digress for a moment and assess the situation. I did not want to be confined to the house nor be in bed for eight months. I also did not want to carry a baby that may not make it full term. Making this decision was not easy for me. I finally settled myself and decided to listen to my husband. As we(he) prayed about it and believed God for a healthy baby, I began to believe too. My heart softened. I began to feel compassion and concern for the health of our baby.

No one could have ever told me that my pregnancy would be filled with so many challenges. I was sick every day. I couldn't hold anything down. Instead of gaining weight, I was losing weight rapidly. I was 98 pounds. It was different than I had imagined. I was entirely unprepared for the level of physical, emotional, and psychological pain I would endure. Instead of feeling joy and excitement in anticipation of our child, I was battling overwhelming feelings of anxiety, resentment, and bitterness.

Like the Azalea, I was withering. I wanted to give up. Spring was coming, and I would soon experience the beauty of my full bloom.

Our Gift, My Bloom

On June 3, 1997, I delivered a healthy baby boy. I gave birth to one of the most talented, amazing, and beautiful gifts in the world if I must say so myself. My husband was so delighted to have a son. We decided to name him after both of our grandfathers, Ishmael Elijah. We felt honored that God chose us to be his parents and prepare him for life in this world.

Our son is now 23 years old, and I have been with his father for a total of 34 years. In that time, I have evolved as a woman. Before I could embrace the gifts of marriage and family, I had to first find myself and learn to love myself.

When I did the work, I began to see myself bloom. I went from a dried up, withering flower to a flower in full bloom.

The biggest lesson that I learned is that GOD KNOWS BEST. We think we know what we want, but it is His purposes that bring us joy. Proverbs 19:21(NIV) says: Many are the plans in a person's heart, but it is the LORD's purpose that prevails. We can have plans for our life, but God has the masterplan. Trust Him. Yield to Him and see your life BLOOM.

My name is Barbara Annette Patterson, and I will continue to BLOOM wherever I am planted.

Meet Barbara Patterson

Barbara is owner of Maximum Assurance Cleaning Service (MACS) located in Hilton Head Island, SC. Integrity, love and excellence are guiding principles in her business of 22 years. She is beloved in her community, with her clients often showering her with lavish surprises and gifts.

Barbara is also an Independent Beauty Consultant with Mary Kay Cosmetics. Her passion is helping women develop and grow. She has built a successful team and is months away from becoming a Director in the organization.

Email: BarbaraPatterson888@gmail.com
Phone: 843-338-6368

CARMEN RUSH

*A Stargazer Lily represents passion,
commitment and determination.*

*I chose this flower because I love the brightness and
beauty of the flower along with its strong fragrant
aroma when it's in bloom. In the stargazer's demise the
scent becomes unfavorable, however its beauty remains.
It's able to withstand the heat and seasons, and always
comes back. These attributes relate to my experiences of
loss and trauma in my life.*

Chapter 7

Blooming in the Midst of Loss
Carmen Rush

I've heard people say, "you don't get to choose the family you are born into," but what if your family had the opportunity to "choose you?" Adoption is a great option when in the middle of chaos. Unfortunately, it results from a loss, and losses can have a significant impact on an individual. My adoptive father was an African American AME Zion pastor and teacher in the south. My adoptive mother was a Caucasian Nurse.

This was my parent's second marriage. They both lost their first set of children in divorce. Being a couple in an interracial marriage in the '70s was not easy, especially in the south. They moved from Texas to my father's birth state North Carolina. My mother, who grew up in Tennessee, lost her whole family after marrying an African American man. Their desire to have a family led them to adoption.

They adopted two multi-racial girls. As I reflect as an adult, I know my mother, with all the best intentions in her heart, was trying to fill a void. I later learned in life that she was adopted. After her first divorce, her son was raised by her adoptive mother. I am sure she thought adopting daughters of her own would fill that pain. During my elementary years, my mother decided to separate from my father. She left us in his care. My father did the best he could raising two multi-racial girls. Doing our hair was the hardest. He finally got the skill of braiding and ponytails. It would take the longest for him to braid two plaits, and then

71

he would threaten me by saying, "you better not be late for school," after he was to blame!

My father was well respected and known in the community for his work. He was strict. He raised us to love ourselves and be respectful of others. We were taught to be mindful of our behavior around others, especially men.

We were not allowed to get our ears pierced or wear pantyhose, which we called stockings. We were to stay in our role as children. It would have killed my father to know that I lost my innocence to a child predator.

While playing outside on our swing set, a stranger stopped and asked me to meet him down on the corner. He said if I did, he would give me a quarter. I was not aware of stranger danger. All the adults at that time in my life were pleasant.

I walked down to the corner to an empty building and found this man with the quarter. He wanted me to do something for him. I knew in my mind and heart that something was not right. I was afraid, but I followed his instructions hoping that he would allow me to leave safely. After he was done, I left with my quarter. When I returned home, I was afraid to tell anyone about the quarter. I hid it in the dirt by the swing set.

I did not understand what happened to me. I was afraid. I feared getting in trouble for doing something bad. In my young mind, I was mad at the strange man. I was also mad with my parents. They were in the house and did not come to look for me. That day, I lost my innocence, a quarter, and the ability to trust people. I began to adopt the mindset of taking care of myself, for no one else would.

My father died of cancer when I was eleven. I needed my mother to get through everything. She was emotionally unavailable. Her response to me was, "why are you calling me?" My parents were separated. My mother had begun living in a nursing facility due to having a stroke. I was aware that she had suffered brain damage from the stroke, but I was confused. Did she not love me enough to console me in my brokenness and pain?

My focus turned to my sister. I was afraid of losing her. I didn't know where we would go. The only thing that mattered to me was that we stay together. I could not handle losing her through all this.

These monumental life experiences would shape the woman I would become. As humans, we crave love and security. Throughout the different phases of my life, I desired these basic needs. At times, I abandoned my values and morals to fulfill the sense of love and connection. It became a self-survival mechanism of sorts.

My younger self did not understand loss. I did not recognize the impact it had on my emotions or decisions. I learned early in life that you cannot depend on your parents to be there for you. Not only had I lost my first set of parents, but also the parents who chose me through adoption. From an early age, I learned to protect and care for myself. My goal was to go to college and become self-sufficient. I never wanted to be dependent again.

My aunt raised me, who made the ultimate sacrifice to raise two children that were not her own. I will forever respect her. She did the best she could despite the odds. However, I now know why my father tried to make an alternate plan for my sister and me.

Due to our dependency, a fear of losing my sister, and fear of losing control, I encountered many difficult and painful situations. I became a victim of physical and sexual abuse and a witness to domestic violence. I also fell prey to alcoholism. Everything I was going through, I kept to myself.

I prayed and told myself that it would be just a matter of time, and I could get myself and sister out of this. At least we were together, right? Suffering this kind of trauma as a child was another loss. I experienced a loss of security, a loss of faith, a loss of childhood, and a loss of self. I chose to allow these life experiences to motivate me. I was determined to become someone better than my life circumstances.

My desire to be liked and loved by everyone grew immensely. I became a people pleaser at an early age. I allowed the fear of loss to play out in all my relationships. Whether it was a friendship or romantic relationship, I would hold on for dear life, even if they were unhealthy.

I was not particular about my partners because I was hungry for love. I married in my mid-twenties, hoping that my husband would fill my void. I soon realized I put too much pressure on my marriage to fill a void.

I began to search for my birth parents. Being a multi-racial adoptee in the south, I knew there would be challenges. I longed for the truth. I was blessed to be reunited with my biological mother and father. In my heart, I just knew this would be the "fix" to my emotional needs.

Upon meeting my birth mother, there was an instant connection between us. I began to feel a level of love and acceptance that I would never forget. Through our reconnection, I was able to connect with my biological father.

Soon after reconnecting with my biological parents, I met my extended family. I had more sisters, brothers, relatives than I could have ever imagined.

Fulfilling this void gave me a sense of unconditional love from my family. I hoped that it would be enough for me emotionally. As time went on, I realized I still did not feel the emotional security I desired. This was not the fix.

I eventually lost my first marriage to divorce. I found myself by myself, which was another long-term fear I had. I called myself a "social butterfly" to cover up the fact that I was too afraid to be alone.

Unbeknownst to me, I began to associate being alone with being unloved. I found myself in a relationship with a man that I knew from the beginning was not right. I ignored all the red flags. Over time, I began to lose a part of myself. I became a slave to finding happiness in someone else.

I began to distance myself from my family and friends. I made excuses for all the hurt. I did not want the relationship to end, but God saw different. He intervened, and the relationship was over.

During this time in my life, both my biological parents died. They passed away within months of each other. I felt so blessed for the years I was able to have them in my life.

At this moment, I found myself alone. I took the time to focus on myself and my faith. I believed in God and knew he was looking out for me. The energy I would give to a man, I turned into myself and God. The more I practiced my faith, the happier I became. God began blessing me in every area of my life.

Out of nowhere, when I least expected it, God allowed a new man to come into my life. I was not looking for love this time. Love was looking for me, and that is a big difference.

Of course, when doors are opening for you, the devil gets mad and tries his best to break you in your weakest areas. As I began to move on and rebuild my life, I became a victim of domestic violence.

The man God moved out of my life found it hard to see me happy and thriving. The devil began attacking my life. Before I realized it, I was sitting in a police car. My body ached after hours of abuse. I had been dragged, hit, kicked, punched, choked, spit on, and more, yet I kept telling myself I was fine.

I was mad and disappointed with myself. I was a social worker. I worked with victims of domestic violence on a daily basis. I couldn't see the signs in front of me. I began to hate myself.

I had hit my "rock bottom." I had been so resilient in all the other traumatic events and losses in my life. This time was different though. I was ready to give it up. I felt alone. I had no one. God showed me different.

My sister and her family were there for me. She helped me re-build my confidence. She wouldn't let me give up on everything I worked so hard for. My new relationship was over. So, I thought. God showed me differently.

When God sends you a real man, one who loves you in a way that you have always prayed for, you notice. That man will love you even when you don't love yourself. He will require you to grow in a manner where you find that love in God and yourself.

For that reason and many others, he is now known as my husband. Amidst all of this, like the old church folks say, "Somebody Prayed for Me." In one of the lowest moments of my life, when I questioned everything, God was still there for me.

Through my many life experiences, I have learned that you will incur loss. It takes time to heal. You must acknowledge the loss and come to grips with the changes. In those moments of loss, I encourage you to learn more about yourself. Learn your purpose and passion so you can drive what happens in your life. Be patient, calm, and resilient. Be self-aware; let the circumstance go mentally and build positive emotions.

Love does not hurt. Yes, your growth may be painful, but love does not hurt. When someone loves you, they show you they care about your feelings.

You are responsible for your happiness, do not look for happiness in others. Don't allow others to have control over your emotions. As an adoptee, I have learned that reconnecting with lost family members does not heal the primal disruption. Always know that the love you seek comes from within and a higher being.

My resilience comes from my faith in God and His son Jesus. I know He will never leave me or forsake me. Every loss and traumatic experience in my life has been a lesson learned. I have become the person I am because of my faith. It has allowed me to bloom into the strong woman I am today. In every season, there is continued growth; God's not through with me yet.

My name is Carmen Rush, and I will continue to BLOOM wherever I am planted.

Meet Carmen Rush

Carmen Rush is a Social Worker and has worked over 24 years in the field of Child Welfare. She received her bachelor's and master's degrees in Social Work, and has a strong passion working with children and families. Carmen has held a leadership position in her Social Work career well over 15 years. Carmen is also a small business owner as an Independent Consultant with Paparazzi Accessories, where she holds the status of Director and leads a team of consultants. She is a native of North Carolina, and currently resides in Atlanta, Georgia with her husband Darron Rush.

Carmen learned the tough lessons of grief, loss, and being resilient, after losing her parents at a young age. As an adoptee, a survivor of domestic violence, neglect, and sexual abuse these life experiences have made Carmen who she is today. Carmen believes that regardless of your circumstances, environment, weaknesses, failures, or bad decisions, you can recover and BLOOM into a beautiful, stronger, radiant, more colorful and fresher YOU, all while planting seeds in others to help them grow and BLOOM at their peak.

Website: www.paparazziaccessories.com/70079
Email: www.cnt0731@gmail.com

DEBRA MARKS

*A tulip represents truth, depth
and undying love.*

*Just like the tulip, a perfect love needs nurturing.
Given the right conditions and care, by planting the
bulb in the fall before the freeze, tulips get busy
preparing for a beautiful emergence in the spring.
Not only does a beautiful, brilliant flower emerge,
underground, but it is also birthing another bulb
for the next generation.*

*In the same way, God's perfect love allows power
through pain for the next generation. My story has
some painful truth; however, it has allowed me to
impart some wisdom to the next generation.*

Chapter 8

The Perfect Love
Debra K. Marks

It was Thursday, March 28, 1991. I was in the office at the bank, along with my co-worker Lisa. We were both Personal Banking Processors. Lisa focused on loans, and I focused on new accounts. Lisa and I often worked a little later, processing the day's work. I was 5 1/2 months pregnant. I experienced morning sickness from day one, but this "morning sickness" was all day nausea.

Eldwin and I lived in a small apartment. We were in our third year of marriage and wanted to buy a house. Eldwin's parents owned the house next door and offered to sell it to us. Eldwin and I prepared to make the purchase, in the meantime, we conceived. I became very ill. Thinking I had the flu, we proceeded with our move.

Well, our house wasn't ready, so we moved in with Mom and Dad. As I stated, I was quite ill, but we continued with the plans. I took a pregnancy test. We were having a baby!

Most days, I was nauseous, but I would go to work. I had a manager, Jan Goldammer. On my worse days, I would call Jan to tell her I just couldn't make it into the office. She would say, "throw up, eat crackers, get ready for work, and I will see you when you arrive!"

I entered my fifth month of pregnancy in March. Wow! I was beginning to feel somewhat better. My nausea had eased up. I told Jan; my goal was to make it to work every day that month. God knew Jan was the best manager for me. She went right along in agreement with my plan. No feeling sorry for me. The last working day of the month was upon us. It was Thursday, March 28! One more day and my goal would come to fruition with success. I was determined!

After the bank closed at 5 pm, Lisa and I had a few things to finish processing the day's work. As I walked to Lisa's desk, I felt cramping. I got to her desk, just in time to grab it. I bent over in pain. I called for Lisa, and she asked if I was ok. I advised her that I was fine. I insisted she go ahead and leave.

Lisa began to leave for the day. The pain happened again. It was more intense than the last. The pain was fifteen minutes apart. After a while, Lisa remained by my side. I started to feel better.

As I approached my car, I almost began to fall to my knees in pain. I told Lisa; it's happening again. She decided to drive me home. As the pain subsided, I told Lisa that Eldwin plays darts on Thursday nights. It was safe to go home. I drove home in discomfort. By the time I arrived home, I could barely move. I didn't tell anyone about my pain.

I cleaned up the house a bit and called Ma. We made plans to go to the grocery store. During the car ride, I told her what was happening. She warned me that it could be false labor. Within twenty minutes of shopping, I was in more pain.

I tried my best to push through the pain. I left my mom inside the store to continue grocery shopping. When my mom returned to the car, I was in tears with pain. She calmly put the groceries in the car and drove.

My mom is amazing! She probably hadn't driven a stick shift car in years, but she went right into "Mom Mode" and did what she needed to do! Ma said, "I'll take you home, and you can get your car later."

When we got to my house, I went to the bathroom. I said, "Ma, I think there is more than urine. I think I'm bleeding." She said, "Let me see." She calmly checked the toilet and went to the linen closet for a sanitary napkin. She continued in her calm voice, "it's not a lot of blood, but I'm taking you to the hospital."

She whisked me off to the hospital. Since my physician was associated with a far-east hospital, she thought it best to go there. Even though Ma was driving quite fast, she told me everything was going to be ok. "Just talk to me and let me know if you are in any pain and stay calm."

When we arrived at the ER, my mom talked to the receptionist. I'm not sure what she said, but they got me in right away! By now, it was well into the evening. My mom contacted Eldwin and other family members. Everyone arrived at the hospital. The doctors concluded I was in preterm labor and started an IV to stop it.

The hospital tried all night to reach my doctor. When he finally arrived on Friday morning, he examined me further. He panicked and began cursing at everyone! "Get the helicopter!!" he cried. He was yelling other commands and things that were too hard to understand. Twenty-nine years later, I still have a scar on the top of my hand, where he was trying to get another IV started. He was shaking so bad it made a huge bruise and scar.

Everyone scurried around, trying to follow his demands. The helicopter departed with another patient. My doctor demanded they get me to Rockford Memorial Hospital NOW!! They rushed me into an ambulance.

An ER Nurse got in with me. She held her face next to my face. As the sirens were going and the driver speeding down State Street, the nurse tried to get me to talk to her. I asked if she thought I was going to die. I could feel her warm tears as they rolled down her face. "If I die, it's ok, I'm ready," I assured her.

At the same time, my sister, Angel, was having a massage. During her massage, my sister could feel my pain. She immediately sat up and told the massage therapist she had to leave now! Angel jumped in her car and rushed to Rockford. The Holy Spirit directed her to Rockford Memorial Hospital!

The paramedics rushed me into the ER. They began to run an emergency ultrasound. They asked me questions about my medical history. I let them know of the excruciating pain I'd been experiencing throughout my pregnancy. The first doctor didn't take me seriously. He just called it "pregnancy."

On the next visit, I expressed it; the doctor told us we were having twins! Eldwin and I were excited! Twins! Wow! The pain seemed to worsen; therefore, my husband and I went to see him again before our regularly scheduled visit. The doctor listened and frowned. He did an ultrasound and told us; I had a bilateral uterus. He explained I had two openings in my uterus. Eldwin and I hadn't heard of this; therefore, we were quite concerned. The doctor said he would keep a close eye on it, but not to worry.

The doctor was wrong. During the ultrasound, I was asked if I had a history of fibroids. I did. My mom, sister, and aunts all had a history of fibroids. They informed me that I had large fibroid tumors. The tumors were pushing the baby out. I also had a condition called placenta previa. The placenta was in front of the baby, which caused the bleeding.

Suddenly, doctors were all around me. The anesthesiologist introduced herself and instructed me to give my rings to my husband. She was very kind and loving, but to the point. She said your husband is going to kiss you and *we hope to see you again.* My husband kissed me with tears rolling down his face.

Dr. Kalchbrenner was at my feet. He introduced himself and the other doctors that would assist him. He told me I had several large fibroid tumors that he would NOT be able to remove. His focus was on getting the baby and saving my life; however, he told us not to expect to wake up to a baby, he/she probably wouldn't make it.

He asked if I had any questions. I said, "YES! I DO! Dr. Kalchbrenner!" Get those fibroids out of me! I exclaimed! He said, Debra, I can't, we'll have to get them later. I repeated it. He said, Debra, you will be asleep in a minute, is there anything else before you go to sleep! I said, yes, one more thing. He said, yes, Debra, I said, Dr. Kalchbrenner, "You are absolutely gorgeous!" Dr. Kalchbrenner and the rest of the team went up in laughter!

I awakened in a short time, to a room full of nonstop laughter. Dr. Kalchbrenner was smiling as he delivered great news. My husband and I had a living handsome baby boy, whom I would see soon. He also said, Debra, we got all of the fibroid tumors out! Everything went very well and fast. They are large, and you can see them, but we got them! He and his team were amazed!

Now, this is an expression of God's Magnificent Perfect Love! God kept me alive, brought a healthy baby boy into the world, and showed an entire medical team His loving miracles. He also gave Dr. Kalchbrenner another reason to continue passionately practicing in the NICU.

I'm sure it's seldom a patient tells the doctor how handsome he is, let alone at a time as critical as that. However, God divinely intervened and used me to bring laughter and joy into a room of doubt and sadness. They were able to look at the challenge at hand with lightheartedness, and I became someone they cared about in a new way.

This is God's, Perfect Love. Just like the blooming of a tulip in the early spring! When it emerges, it brings joy, a smile, and a mysterious peace. We all await their springtime blooming.

Our son, Eldwin L. Marks II, lived for three days. He was born Good Friday. He went to be with our Lord and Savior, Jesus Christ, Easter Monday. Psalms 145:3 reads: *Great is The Lord, and greatly to be praised, and His greatness is unsearchable.* God used our little guy to bless so many! God continued to show us and many others His miracles!

Easter Monday, my supervisor and friend, Jan Goldammer, visited me at the hospital. She gave me the biggest hug while we reminisced about the last three days. We laughed about my determination to get to work even up to the last minute, during the ambulance ride. We laughed until we cried!

The nurse came to get Eldwin and me to see our sweet little guy, one more time. Little Eldwin had begun to bleed through his skin. They knew it would be his last day on earth. We talked to him, cried, and the nurses told us he was crying too.

They had monitors on him that showed his movement. We were unable to see his tears because his tear ducts were underdeveloped. Every time we visited him, he responded vigorously to our voices, especially Eldwin's. We released him into the almighty hands of God. When he perished, they unhooked all of the wires from his tiny body, wrapped him in a blanket, and allowed us to hold him. Oh, so sweet and gone so soon!

The funeral director came to our house as we began to make burial plans. Within just a few days, we stood graveside in Sunset Memorial Gardens Babyland to say our final earthly good-byes until we meet again.

Our family was right by our side! All four of our parents, our grandparents, our siblings, and even some of our aunts. It's incredible what expressions of emotions Eldwin II brought to the surface. My Mom and Dad, who had separated, but remained friends, held each other to bring comfort to each other. Eldwin's Mom and Dad also lovingly help each other find comfort. Our sisters, Angel and Lynn, and our brothers Dean and Michael shed tears of sorrow as they mourned the nephew, they thought they would hold. Grandpa and Grandma Jones and Auntie Van hugged us as we cried together.

Our Pastor, Bishop Washington, officiated the service. We were all brought together, just like a bouquet of tulips for one purpose. We celebrated the three days God used our son to show unconditional love! Just like our Heavenly Father to express such Perfect Love through our baby boy!

The next eight weeks would prove to be quite the test! Eldwin and I had to go home without our baby. Other than a follow-up doctor's appointment, I stayed in bed. I was depressed. My sister Angel and Joy Lambert sent flowers. I can still see and smell the dozens of yellow roses and tulips that graced our home. My beautiful Ma came over daily with food.

My honey went back to work after two weeks. It was hard for Eldwin. As a quiet man, he never complained. However, he came home daily to a depressed, weepy wife, who had not attempted to get up.

During this recovery time, Eldwin came home one day and said, "You are not the only one grieving. I lost my son too." He emphasized. "Now, get up!" This push was the best thing he could have done for me for us. We sought out counseling. We had some laughs and shed some tears.

If you had asked me if I was blooming, I would have laughed. I was blooming. Indeed, I was.

Our third-year anniversary was June 4, 1991, just a couple of months after our son's birth. My sweet, loving, and kind husband planned the most beautiful anniversary celebration for us. When we returned, we were in a much better place emotionally. Within a week or so, I was experiencing severe nausea. Each morning, I began waking up to a dash to the bathroom to barf. I thought, mmm..."Could it be?" "Already? No, we are using protection!"

I attempted to go back to the same doctor on the east side. I was unsuccessful. God knew! My sister, Lynn Penix, expressed to Dr. Washington, I needed a new doctor. He said his practice was full. She begged him until he said yes. During my first visit with Dr. Washington, he told me to continue to see Dr. Kalchbrenner. I would need high-risk care.

Dr. Kalchbrenner gave us our choices; abortion or abortion. He expressed to me the baby wouldn't make it through another pregnancy. He showed us the fibroids on the ultrasound. They were larger than the baby. We told Dr. Kalchbrenner, we were going to pray. He said," you don't understand. You will not make it." He insisted that we schedule an abortion. We left without scheduling it.

One Sunday morning, while at church, I walked down the hall before service. Mother McGee, affectionately known as Nana, was coming toward me. She put her items down and said; I must pray NOW! She began to pray, laying hands on me and speaking in tongues.

At the next doctor's appointment, I had an ultrasound. This one would prove God's, Perfect Love! As doctor Kalchbrenner was moving the wand over my belly, he said just a minute. He called in another physician. They all looked at my stomach, amazed. Eldwin and I said, "What do you see?" With a perplexed look on his face, Dr. Kalchbrenner told us the fibroids were gone. I threw my hands up and shouted, "Praise the Lord! "The doctors gave us a scientific reason. God created science, and God created man. Yes, a scientific miracle took place when Nana prayed for me. To God Be The Glory! Perfect Love!

Our beautiful daughter, Kayana Renee' Marks, was born March 26, 1992, three days before Little Eldwin almost a year later. Our miracle baby is 28 years young and will become a physician. Our handsome son, Jonathan Lewis Marks, was born June 21, 1994, three months after his brother and sister two years later. Our second miracle son lives in Washington DC and is an entrepreneur.

My story embodies the circle of life. It began at the office, to the birth, to the graveside, and back to a new birth. Most have biological, church, adoptive, and office families. My story depicts God's perfect love through all of these families coming together. Somewhat like a bouquet of tulips of many colors. While creating a beautiful, refreshing, life-enhancing addition to its environment, it expresses God's, Perfect Love. My story also exposes my innocence and ignorance.

My message to the next generation is to take your time when selecting a doctor. You must interview him/her. Do your homework, know their reputation. You must know what questions you should ask. Every person is important and deserves to be heard and respected.

A real lesson from this part of my journey is to embrace every experience life brings. You must listen to your inner voice and glean from other resources. Ecclesiastes 3:2 says, a time to be born and a time to die. Yes, we shall all surely die.

A mother doesn't imagine burying her child. The reality is that it rains on the just and the unjust. We must build our house on a solid foundation, Jesus Christ. When we do that, we can withstand the trials and tribulations of life!

Receive God's Love, live the abundant life, and Bloom!

My name is Debra K. Marks, and I will continue to BLOOM wherever I am planted.

Meet Debra Marks

Debra is a Speaker, Entrepreneur and Evangelist. For over 20 years Debra has focused on helping people achieve optimal health--physically, emotionally, financially, and spiritually. Her passion to see others healthy and free has allowed her to impact thousands through the products and services offered in her small business ventures.

Debra believes that helping others achieve optimal health is a ministry and mandate from God, for which she remains focused and undeterred. She is an active member of her church and her greatest desire is to fulfill God's plan for her life.

Debra is a Corporate Coordinator for BetterLife Wellness at Swedish American Hospital in Rockford, Illinois and is the owner of YOU, a personal assistant company. She is happily married to her childhood sweetheart, Eldwin Marks, and from their union of 31 years came 3 wonderful children: Eldwin II, now in heaven and two adult children, Kayana and Jonathan.

Email: debra.marks03@yahoo.com
Phone: 815-243-3380

DEBRA MITCHELL

A purple tulip represents royalty, true, deep and undying love.

My flower is a passionate purple tulip. The process of creating purple is very lengthy, expensive and requires a lot of hard work. Just like the purple tulip, blooming into a Diva with Standards requires a lot of hard work.

Chapter 9

I'm a Diva with Standards!
Debra Clifton Mitchell

A Diva in Training

I grew up with my maternal grandmother, parents and three older sisters. My sisters are close in age. However, I am 11 years younger and often felt like I didn't belong. Not only was I much younger, but I also had nothing in common with my siblings. My sisters did not like young children. I was proof of this. Whenever I went anywhere with them, it was because they were forced to take me by mother. Dragging their kid sister with them was a real Debbie Downer – no pun intended.

Growing up, I was exposed to lots of promiscuity. By the time I was in the 2nd grade, I had seen and heard much more than any child should. I saw boys in the alleys with girls in various sex acts. Whenever I was forced to with my sisters, I knew I would be around a bunch of horny teenagers. By the end of the day, I would hear and see things that are classified as X-rated and not suitable for children. As a result, I had no interest in boys or premarital sex. For my perspective, they just used women. These experiences caused me to want to do better and be a person that lived with high morals and values. I was determined to be different and a lot of that was because of my grandmother.

I didn't know it back then, but I used my love for reading to cope with these situations. Whenever I was forced to go with my sisters, I always had a backpack full of books I borrowed from the library. I would read books as a distraction to the sights and sounds around me. I would travel to exotic places as they came alive on the pages. I became very disciplined and excelled in school. When I graduated from high school, I was ranked number three and had perfect attendance for all four years.

My grandmother was my protector and had the most influence in my life. I can remember her telling me, "You're not going to be like your sisters, I'm not going to let you go down the wrong road." She knew all the negative influences that were around me that would have diminished my future. Based on everything I saw, I made up my mind at that very moment that I would not allow men to degrade, use or abuse me. I was worthy of much more. I was Diva in Training!

Turning Points

Now my mother was an overbearing strong-willed woman. She was also very manipulative. She had a, *my way or the highway attitude*. She controlled my three sisters. She actually handicapped them and was very critical. They were unhappy and acted accordingly. None of them ever stood up to her and they did things to hurt and embarrass her and the family. By the time I was in 6th grade, I became wise beyond my years and quickly understood that *hurt people hurt people*. She even controlled them from the grave. It took many years after her death for them to finally live the lives that they wanted.

However, I made a different choice regarding my mom. I stood up to her. I believe this helped me gain self-confidence and independence. She often told anybody she encountered that "Debra is not like my other girls." She meant this in a negative way, however, I took it as a compliment. She could not control me.

The first time I stood up to her I was in the 8th grade. I refused to attend the neighborhood high school like my sisters. I took the entrance exam and was accepted into a

94

magnet school across town. I had to take two buses each way to get to school. She told me that I was required to attend college in my hometown.

Again, I refused. I applied to Illinois State University and lived on campus earning my Bachelor's of Science in Business Administration. I earned a Master's of Business Administration in Business Administration and two other advanced designations. This fall, I am pursuing my Ph.D. in Business and Psychology with a specialization in Counseling Psychology. As part of my commitment to make mental health services available to all women, I will provide counseling sessions on a pro bono basis.

When I got engaged, my mother wanted me to get married at the church that I grew up in, which is a United Methodist church. My fiancée is a member of a Baptist church. We decided to get married at his church and I planned to join his church right after our honeymoon. My mother advised me that she wasn't going to attend the wedding if I didn't get married at the United Methodist church.

I was not deterred and wasn't going to let her run or ruin my life. I asked my dad if he would walk me down the aisle and give me away. He was very supportive and commended me for wanting to get married instead of shacking up. He also agreed with me and felt that a wife should follow her husband and worship together. This of course, is different than what my parents did. He advised that he would be honored to give me away and that I always made him proud.

Even though I was the youngest in the family, I had no problem standing up for myself or others. I believe it was because of the dysfunction I was exposed to as a child. My sisters admired me for standing up to our mother. I became the leader of the pact, even though I was over a decade younger. In fact, my dad made me his power of attorney after my mom died.

In The Dark With No Flashlight

No one ever talked about anything of any value or to prepare me for life when I left home. I never got lessons on how to manage my finances, career choices or healthy relationships. Also, there were no good examples of happily married couples, even in my extended family.

On my 18th birthday, my grandmother asked me what I thought my life would be like in the next ten years. I told her I was going to finish college, obtain an advanced degree, secure a leadership position in corporate America and live in a condo downtown. She asked me "What about a husband and children?" I responded by stating, "That's not in the cards for me. I've not met one happily married couple and I refuse to be a statistic – a single mom with a deadbeat dad or kids by multiple men."

She understood and was devastated at the same time. She told me all girls are supposed to grow up, get married and have children. She had four children and my mother had four children. She was counting on me to have four children. I had to explain to her that the tradition was going to be broken. All I had seen were women that were hurt, damaged, lost and self-destructive. She told me that meant that I had not met my Mr. Right. She prayed for me and told me that hoped she would live long enough to see me get married and have a family of my own.

Because I witnessed so much promiscuity, I really took a long time selecting my husband. I continued to pray to God to send me the man he had created just for me. I believe everybody has a perfect match, just like Adam and Eve. I set the standards very high for my future husband. When I was a college freshman, I met my future husband. He was my only boyfriend and we dated eight years before we got married. My grandmother would often ask me when I planned to marry this young man. She told me, *He's a keeper!* When she gave her seal of approval, I knew he was the one.

I expressed my apprehension about getting married to my fiancée several times. He knew my family history. He reassured me by stating *Just because their marriages didn't make it, doesn't mean our marriage can't make it. I'm in it for the long haul.* He even asked my dad and mom for my hand in marriage. As a result of this lack of training, I knew I would have to learn on my own how to have a successful and happy marriage. Love would not be enough. This was very scary! At that time, I understood why the divorce rate is so high. I would have to do things completely opposite of what I saw growing up.

I had to learn to *talk to my husband and not about him* to others. He and I were a team. I had to pick my battles and think about which issues were worth discussing and which ones were not. It is impossible to debate about "everything."

I, like most people, am a creature of habit. I learned to take time to reflect on what occurred during difficult times and make mental notes so I could avoid the pitfalls in the future. I know how to push my husband's buttons, but realize it is unnecessary to get my point across.

Nobody is perfect, so I don't hold grudges or live in the past. Instead, I look forward to the future and growing old with my husband. I still want him to be excited to come home every day and create new memories.

It's been 34 years now since I married the love of my life, a grand total of 42 years together! My grandmother finally got her wish. She lived long enough to see me get married and have both of my children. (My daughter was even born on her birthday!) Through her sacrifice, prayers and determination, my grandmother was able to see me evolve into a Diva with Standards. I grew into a confident woman who understands her worth, A woman who followed her own path and became the best version of herself. I am grateful for my grandmother's influence and consistent guidance. She was truly a gift from God!

My Message to The Next Generation

It's been said that we are the average of the five people we spend the most time with. The people we hang around with will shape our attitudes and behaviors. That being said, my message to you is to choose wisely. Set your sights high. Seek to understand your purpose. Set goals for yourself and never succumb to a negative environment.

My name is Debra Clifton Mitchell and I will continue to BLOOM wherever I am planted.

Meet Debra Mitchell

Debra Mitchell is an Award-Winning Author, Motivational Speaker and Life Coach. Her first book "How to Find The Right Man and Become His Center of Attention" received numerous literary awards and honorable mentions, as well as her other two books that followed. They are now known as *The Healthy Relationships Trilogy Books for women of all ages.*

Debra is passionate about helping women make better choices when it comes to relationships and marriage. She has successfully mentored and taught thousands of women on how to find a great relationship, keep it alive and beat the odds.

Debra has been happily married for 34 years to Dwayne Mitchell, Sr and together they are the proud parents of two adult children, Danielle and Dwayne Jr. She has a Bachelor's and Master's Degree in Business Administration. She is currently pursuing her Ph.D. in Business and Psychology with a specialization in Counseling Psychology. As part of her commitment to make mental health services available to all women, she plans to offer pro bono counseling services.

She is a native of Chicago, Illinois and a Diamond Life Member of Delta Sigma Theta Sorority, Inc.

Email: Debramitchell78@yahoo.com
Phone: 708-807-1136

DOROTHY DAVIS

A deep pink rose represents gratitude, appreciation, and recognition.

The rose analogy represents the stages that changed my life. The rosebud applies to my innocence in my earlier childhood. The prickles are the traumas I experienced growing up. The petals are the bright moments that helped build my adaptability to life's struggles.

Chapter 10

Transitions of a Rose
A. Dorothy Davis

The Rosebud- An unopened flower. Innocence.

When I was five years old, I lived the life of a storybook princess. I lived in a big house with a huge backyard. My grandmother had a flower garden that I loved to play in. My grandmother, my mom, and my aunt were like queens. My grandfather was the king and our house was the castle. Our second home was the red brick church building. This is where we spent several days of the week attending Sunday services, prayer meetings, choir rehearsals, and special events.

I loved getting dressed up in fancy dresses with lacy slips and patent leather shoes. I was in a fashion show and had a great time. I even had a red tricycle that I rode around our porch.

There were so many happy moments; Easter egg hunts, Christmas speeches, and playing under a quilting table with my best friend Tracey while our grandmothers were quilting with their friends.

I felt God had smiled on me at this time in my life. I was so innocent and joyful. I loved my family. I felt beautiful. God was in His heaven and all was right in my world.

Some of my favorite places to go were church, the library, and the park. My mother took me to these places, and I enjoyed each one of them. The church gave me spirituality, the library gave me knowledge, and the park was my playground.

One of my favorite memories was when my mother read books to me at night before I went to bed. She also combed my hair, tied ribbons on my ponytails, and picked out my clothes (all matching of course) for the next day.

I have read that the first five years form a child's foundation. I want you to see the structure, love, and sense of family that helped me build resilience, and later in my life survive.

Lesson 1- remember your childhood princess moments.

The Thorns - Sometimes called prickles that protect the flower from harm

There were several thorny parts of my life after age seven. There was a fire, my grandmother's death, and my struggle with self-esteem. When I was seven years old, my house caught on fire and burned to the ground while I stood watching clutching my teddy bear and my blanket. The flames destroyed the castle, the beautiful flower garden, and everything we owned. I blacked out as to where we stayed after the fire.

My grandparents bought a smaller house with money my grandmother had inherited from relatives down south. It was several blocks away from our old house. The first prickle was the feelings of abandonment. I no longer had my aunt and my cousins living with us. They moved farther away from us. I was very anxious, and my skin broke out with eczema. I think it was anxiety. I had a horrible rash on my arms and legs. My grandmother blamed it on the wild plants outside, and the shag carpet.

I know now the eczema was a result of not being able to discuss the fire and losing part of my family. It was only the four of us, my grandparents and my mother and me. I was also very lonely without my cousins. I missed sitting on their bed, watching them get dressed for dances and dates. I was lost without my cousin to play hide and seek with me. My grandmother did not plant a flower garden, but she did have a pink rose bush. She also planted a small vegetable garden. I think she missed our old home too.

There were blessings in this new world. I continued to read books and go to the library every week. I still had my best friend and had fun riding my purple bike. I had my church family.

Lesson 2—Even in the darkness, there are joyful moments.

The Second Thorn

School was hard for me. I was short and skinny. I had eczema and people did not want to play with me. I was teased because of my name. I was called Olive Oyl and Aardvark, which is an anteater. I also developed asthma. I couldn't run or play sports, which isolated me. I buried myself in books. The library was my refuge. I was also bullied in middle school.

One terrific thing happened to me. When I was twelve, a revival came to town. I gave my life to Christ. I became more aware of God's love and what it meant to have a personal relationship with Him.

Lesson 3- God can change your life.

The Worst Thorn

When I was fourteen years old, my grandmother died. She had a heart attack on her way to church. It felt like someone pulled the heart out of my chest. No one could help me with my grief. Our small home became a tomb. My grandfather and my mother were both in depression. My grandfather said he wanted to die. He shut down emotionally. I still had my two friends, but I was drowning in pain. I became angrier. My eczema got worse and my asthma was out of control.

In my first year of high school, I had a rough time focusing on work. One rainy, gray day, I walked out of high school intending to kill myself. My plan was not well thought out. I decided to walk in front of a car. I tried to get hit, but the car swerved and missed me by an inch. God had His hands all over my life! I walked a few blocks away to a counseling center. I told the receptionist I needed help. For several years, I was blessed to have had a counselor to help me recover from my grandmother's death. God would not let me give up. I was beginning to see my worth.

Blooming

I have had my share of trials and tribulations. Through it all, God has brought me out and sustained me. I have grown so much in my relationship with the Lord. My scripture is Philippians 4:13, I can do all things through Christ who strengthens me. I have been broken, made mistakes, and felt worthless, however, God loved me through it all. He has given me an amazing family and a great job. I am working on my master's degree in counseling to help other broken people become whole. I am starting a business that will empower women to be marvelous through God's help and love. I am blooming!!

Petals of Wisdom

I have some petals of wisdom for future generations. First, you are amazing! No matter what difficulties you may encounter in life, you are beautiful and blessed by God! Secondly, you can turn life's negatives into positives! You make the choice to decide your perspective on life. Choose to see the good in each day and be grateful. Finally, you can achieve your goals! It may take work and resilience, but you can do it!

My name is Dorothy Davis, and I will continue to BLOOM wherever I am planted.

Meet Dorothy Davis

Resilience is the one word that best describes Dorothy. By her 21st birthday, Dorothy had experienced the loss of her immediate family, battled significant health problems, and met and triumphed over many struggles. "Instead of defeating me, they only served to produce resilience in my life," says Dorothy. "I refuse to succumb to a defeatist, negative view of life. My motto for life is 'Bloom! I can do all things through Christ who strengthens me."

Dorothy earned a bachelor's degree in Psychology and is currently finishing a master's degree in Counseling. She has passionately worked in the social service field for 35 years, helping people overcome adversity, solve problems, and develop resiliency.

Her goal is to use her strengths to empower others to find God's purpose for their lives.

Dorothy has been married for 39 years to the love of her life, Kenneth. They have five adult children and live in central Illinois.

GWENDOLYN MARTIN

A sunflower represents adoration,
and dedication.

Sunflowers are symbols to remind us to follow our
faith, be flexible and seek nourishment. To keep our
marriage stable and growing, it needs nurturing just
like a sunflower. Especially, in times of drought or
excess rain. If we keep our marriage fertilized and
moist with daily gestures of affection, attention,
expressions of gratitude, and open communication, we
will be able to overcome any obstacle our marriage
encounters. Like the sunflower, our love endures, is
timeless and is the essence of our loyalty to each other.

Chapter 11

Granny's Lessons From The Garden
Gwendolyn A. Martin

Enjoying the view: My happy place

Have you ever spent time outside on a stressful day just gazing at the sun or taking in nature's beauty? Picture a wild sunflower field in full bloom with their tall stalks and bright petals stretched towards the sun. Sunflowers are known for being happy flowers, so it is apt that symbolically it belongs in my happy place; my bright, cheery, warm, inviting backyard oasis.

I love being in my backyard. It is so peaceful and serene with its colorful flowers, sights, sounds, smells, and textures. There is a bistro, dining, living, and patio area. Each area has its attractions and therapeutic benefits of mother nature that sustain me from day today. There are times I stay in the backyard all day. It does not matter if I am tending to herbs, pulling weeds, or enjoying a kindle read. Sometimes I sit and blow bubbles, rock in one of the gliders, or sip on a glass of wine while catching up with family and friends.

When I am in the garden, time ceases to exist, and I get immersed in nature's beauty. The restoration and revitalization that my garden brings is a positive, motivating force in my marriage. My husband and I embrace the beautiful garden of love, symbolic of the beautiful life we created over the last twenty years. Like the sunflower, our love endures, is timeless, and is the essence of our loyalty to each other.

Pulling Weeds

In the first eleven years of marriage, we just focused on us. We took frequent weekend trips, planned weeklong vacations, attended concerts, had frequent dinner dates, and just enjoyed each other. We had no kids, so in essence, we were free to just be. In February of two thousand eleven, our lives got turned upside down. My husband and I got a call that his grandmother had fallen and hit her head. We rushed over to check on her. We ended up spending the night and never went back home. It was no longer safe for granny to live alone.

I remember having a conversation with my husband about staying with Granny. He shared that he would stay with Granny, and I could go back home and come stay with them on weekends. We usually checked in on Granny on the weekends anyways. This way, I would not have to make the daily forty-minute commute to work.

He shared how he already worked in town and was accustomed to checking in on granny daily so it would be more convenient for him to stay. Yeah, well, that did not sit well with me; in my mind, that was not how this marriage thing was supposed to work. After all, he had been commuting our entire marriage. There are always choices and priorities. In this instance, I felt that the better option was to stay with my husband and support him in supporting his grandmother. So, overnight we became instant live-in caretakers of his ninety-year-old grandmother. She became the priority.

Life became drastically different when we moved in with Granny. We were in the process of building a home but abruptly abandoned those dreams. We went from the two of us living in a 3-bedroom, 2.5 bath townhouse, to sharing a 3-bedroom, one bath house with Granny. Privacy and some comforts (walking around in your birthday suit) went right out the window. The amenities we had grown accustomed to were radically different. There was no central heat and air.

The house had two window air conditioners. One was in granny's bedroom, and the other was in the living room.

If you know anything about older people, they are always cold and like fresh air. We were accustomed to never turning the air conditioner off and rarely opened the windows. There was a wall unit for heating that put out massive amounts of heat in a short period, and there was no way to regulate it. We just had to turn it on and off. So, regulating the house's temperature with Granny always being cold, my husband being extremely hot-natured, and me falling somewhere in the middle was comical. We had a washing machine but no clothes dryer. There was not even an electrical outlet to support a dryer.

My days consisted of waking up early to wash clothes and hang them out on the clothesline in the backyard. My husband would bring them in on his lunch break. Yeah, I said it, a clothesline. We had no internet service or cable. I went from having a walk-in closet and a guest closet at my disposal to sharing a closet with my husband. We practically lived out of suitcases and storage bins. Our queen-sized bed became a full-size bed in my husband's childhood bedroom. There were many sacrifices and adaptations.

The strength of our marriage was tested during this time. We sold our townhouse about four months after moving in with Granny and moved everything into storage. My life was changing, personally, and professionally. Maintaining a work/life balance was a struggle. Most of my days were spent nurturing distressed students, consulting overwhelmed parents, and meeting with insensitive administrators. During this time, I became a part-time college professor and maintained my role as a full-time school counselor. The professor's role required an additional two-hour commute on the day I taught classes and extra time away from home.

One day a week, I left home at six-thirty in the morning and did not return until around nine or after eleven at night, depending on the number of classes I taught. I was putting in over sixty hours of work a week. I often skipped breakfast, and occasionally skipped lunch. I was always on the run. I survived on snack foods during the day and fast foods at night. There were days I cooked meals at home, but we often opted for the convenience of takeout.

At home, our lives centered around work, household chores, and caring for Granny with little time for friends or family. My success-driven life left little room for rest and self-care. Most of the time, I was running on empty, drained, and exhausted. I was surviving but not thriving. My life was out of balance. As a counselor, I was not practicing what I preached. I was far more adept at recommending self-care to others than finding the time to practice it myself. We were giving more time, energy, and devotion to work and caring for Granny than ourselves or our marriage.

Planting Seeds

While caring for granny, our union became disconnected. One of the things this marital sacrifice revealed was the need to take care while giving care; we needed to nurture ourselves and our marriage. Those spontaneous weekend trips and weeklong vacations that we often spent just reconnecting with each other were not an option during caregiving.

As a result, we decided to create a space in the backyard that would serve as a place where we could escape the daily hustle and bustle, unwind, and reconnect after work. We called it our backyard oasis. If we could not get away to unplug and indulge in emotional bonding, we would bring the vacation destination to us.

The oasis was our alternative self-care solution in response to unhealthy behaviors aligned with the dedication to work and caregiving. It provided a place to bond, de-stress, and bridge the disconnect in our marriage. Time spent creating our outside oasis helped heal my body, mind, and spirit and ultimately strengthened my marriage. We created an environment outside of work and caring for others where we could be soothed and nurtured while spending quality time together. It was not Cancun or the Caymans but served its purpose, nonetheless.

I bloomed through this whole experience. In the beginning, I just bought flowers that looked pretty and planted them wherever in the garden. I did not take the time to learn about the flowers or what they needed to grow and survive. I wasted a lot of time and money. The flowers looked pretty, but only lasted a short time. Some flowers withered and died from too much sun, while others like the calla lily rotted from too much rain. Sunflowers' soil should be watered when the soil's top inch is dry and should be kept moist but not soggy for optimal growth. Sunflowers must be fertilized during the growing season.

To keep our marriage stable and growing, it needs nurturing, just like a sunflower, especially in drought or excess rain. If we keep our marriage fertilized and moist with daily gestures of affection, attention, expressions of gratitude, and open communication, we will be able to overcome any obstacle our marriage encounters. I am firm in my belief that we need to water, feed, fertilize, and plant seeds with optimistic goals and eager expectations of a colorful, vibrant garden. We must engage in these same steps in our marriage for it to thrive. We must protect our garden from harmful creatures like the occasional snake, people, thoughts, actions, and circumstances that can get in the way of remembering what is most important for our relationship to grow, flourish and sustain.

As with any marriage, there will always be obstacles. Therefore, we must pay attention to our own and each other's nurturing needs. I love it when he recognizes that I am tired or not feeling well, and he cooks a full dinner and insists on doing the dishes too. He loves it when he knows I am tired or just do not feel like cooking but put in the extra effort to do so anyway. Sometimes we get in there and do it together.

Although takeout might be convenient, we recognize that it is not the best option, so we indulge sparingly. We often cook with fresh herbs and vegetables like basil, oregano, lemon balm, thyme, rosemary, peppers, and tomatoes, that we grow in the garden. There is something about eating food that you have personally worked to harvest that just makes food taste better. We are mindful of our nutritional needs.

Perhaps it is because we are finally able to heed our self-care advice. I know I am making overcoming marital challenges sound simple, but anyone who has ever been married knows that is not the case. Marriage is a lot of hard work. Marriage takes daily nurturing, and it is easy to let weeds obscure your view of how maintenance can restore your garden's beauty.

We took care of Granny for a year and a half before she quietly slipped away in her sleep at ninety-two. Despite all the sacrifices, the time spent with Granny is some of my most cherished memories. The history lessons about her time spent training as a nurse and lieutenant in the army, sarcastic wit and sense of humor, proactive approach to life, and ability to see the beauty and find joy in seemingly small things profoundly impact my life.

Moving in with Granny turned out to be a blessing in disguise, which has inspired personal growth and professional growth. I learned to navigate, caring for others compassionately, and with mindfulness while balancing competing demands and successfully took an active stance toward healthy alternatives. In one word: "self-care". Sunflowers are symbols to remind us to follow our faith, be flexible, and seek nourishment.

Growth

Sunflowers are symbols of healing. In May of two-thousand seventeen, I got a call that changed my life. My husband and I were outside in the garden planning and sprucing up our oasis for a Mother's Day dinner and surprise birthday party for my sister the following weekend. We took a break to hydrate, and my husband went inside for a refill. He heard my cell phone ringing and informed me when he came out. I had several missed calls from family members in the span of a few minutes.

I soon discovered that my sister had died unexpectedly. Ironically, I was in the garden when I got the shocking news. It is also ironic that I returned to the garden every morning after my sister's death, especially leading up to laying her to rest. It is this connection with nature that fed my spirit and provided the energy I needed daily. Each morning I would wake up and go sit in the garden to cry and pray. This was the quiet time I needed to take care of me. Some days I would sit, wonder, and reflect while other days I walked to get all the nervous energy out. The garden provided a respite where I could heal, recharge, and navigate this terrible loss.

The garden provided the nourishment I needed at the start of each day as I prepared to be a pillar of strength for my family. I would cook or purchase meals for my immediate family daily to ensure they were being nourished and nurtured. The paradigm was already shifting. Cooking for the family was my sister's thing, and she was the nurturer. I remember my niece saying that she could not eat until the day I cooked a pot of soup. That was the one thing she could eat. We buried my sister on her fifty-fourth birthday.

The day after, the immediate family gathered at my house for that Mother's Day dinner to remember my sister and draw strength from each other before everyone dispersed. The garden was where everyone gravitated. I still have a peace lily that someone gifted at the funeral that sits right next to one of the gliders on the patio. It continues to thrive each year, as do the fond memories of my sister. During one of the most challenging times in my life, the garden provided a tranquil place to escape, reflect, and heal.

Full Bloom

Granny's house is now the place we call home. We maintained the home's integrity by restoring and incorporating family heirlooms, like an old daybed and a roll-top desk that belonged to my husband's great-grandfather. His grandmother cherished them. We now love them too. We renovated, modernized, and made the house our own by adding square footage to include enlarged bedrooms, additional bathrooms, walk-in closets, and a large family room. We incorporated modern amenities like central heat and air, a laundry room, and an updated kitchen. It is a blessing that my husband gets to live in the house he grew up in and where we took care of Granny, overcame obstacles, and triumphed as a married couple.

Today, the backyard is my place of peace and tranquility. One of the first things we did was remove the chain-linked fence and replaced it with a white vinyl fence for privacy. We removed the clothesline, added seating areas with concrete pavers, and dug out flower beds. We incorporated beautiful flowers and plants to include ferns, lilies, begonias, geraniums, vincas, succulents, roses, marigolds, daisies, and hibiscus that give the yard a tropical look and feel. There are whimsical little frogs' statues for garden buddies (although I have found my prince) and a few elephants strategically placed in Granny's remembrance. She loved elephants. We also installed electrical outlets to illuminate the yard at night to make it warm, bright, beautiful, usable, and to highlight certain features.

Our oasis is where I feel empowered and go to renew my strength. I invest as much time in our marriage as I do in the garden. I know that I must do things to create and maintain the marriage I dreamed about and desire. I cannot spend a little bit of time nurturing my marriage and expect that it will flourish. Like seeds, a marriage needs water to grow. When we are thirsty, we must drink from the pool of our love for each other, and make sure that the pool never runs dry because of the commitment we promised each other before God, family, and friends.

Like soil, a marriage needs the right nourishment to flourish. Like flowers, a marriage needs sunlight to thrive. We must grow our garden where the flowers get the right amount of light from the sun. Just as sunflowers follow the sun, we must let the sun illuminate our marriage too so that through love, we overcome any obstacles we face on life's journey together. If I stop nurturing my sunflower, it will wither and die. If I want the best for our marriage, we must continuously monitor it and provide the water, nourishment, or sunlight it needs.

We designed our oasis as a place for us, our family, and friends to congregate individually or as a group. We invite people to come and enjoy this place of comfort and healing. There is even a sign that says, *"sit long, talk much, laugh often."* In the best of times, the garden has provided a space to celebrate joyous occasions in our lives. For instance, we have held parties to include my fortieth, my husband's fiftieth, my mom's seventieth, and my dad's seventy-fifth birthday. We have also hosted several holiday gatherings. Christmas parties have become a favorite time to connect with family and friends. We have also had the occasional just because parties...just because it is the spring of the year, just because the weather is nice, just because it will be nice to get everyone together. We always make it a point to invite married couples so that they can reconnect too.

We get a lot of compliments on our yard. I remember a neighbor stopping by one day trying to convince us to let him maintain it. He argued that we work hard and spend all day on Saturdays cleaning the yard. He said we could be spending that time going places and enjoying each other. I just laughed and told him this was our bonding time in addition to exercise and stress relief. It is an important part of our self-care regimen.

We often have friends, family, or guests ask who maintains our yard, and it is always a source of pride when

I smile and tell them we do. So, when our friends and family make positive comments about our garden, I know that our marriage is nourished through loving words and actions and reaping what we sowed. We enjoy the beautiful bloom and fragrant smell of the flowers, the sweet taste of fruits, and the delicious flavors of various vegetables and herbs that we harvest. Our marriage will reap the same metaphorical bounty year after year that our garden does if we are attentive gardeners and partners.

My message is simple; something pretty amazing happens when you put in the time and effort it takes to keep your marriage and garden watered, nourished, and make sure it gets the proper sunlight – it flourishes.

My name is Gwendolyn Martin, and I will continue to BLOOM wherever I am planted.

Meet Dr. Gwendolyn Martin

Dr. Gwendolyn Martin, who goes by the name Dr. Gwen is a passionate, hard-working, devoted teacher, counselor and former college professor. She has dedicated her career to working with some of the most vulnerable, challenging and high needs populations.

The work is demanding, sometimes frustrating, and often emotional. She has learned over the past 23 years that if she doesn't establish effective self-care, health and wellness routines, the potential for professional burnout is huge.

Dr. Gwen is a leading expert and authority creating high level research-based programs in the areas of self-care, health and wellness. Her education, experiences and entrepreneurial pursuits have led the way for her current project, Dr. Gwen's Counselor Cafe. This platform will provide effective solutions for helping professionals, to include educators, school counselors and licensed clinicians.

Dr. Gwen has served in several professional capacities to champion her work. She has one very important mission in mind and that is to support and empower helping professionals in finding a healthy balance professionally, physically, mentally and spiritually. She believes you must practice what you preach for longevity and sustainability in helping professions. Dr. Gwen has embraced her role as helper and is constantly evolving in the practice of self-care.

JANICE BARNWELL

A carnation represents pride, beauty
and suffering.

Like the carnation, I am from a culture that is filled
with pride and beauty. We are the Gullah people.
Strong, spiritual, resilient, and powerful.
All of this, I am and will continue to be.

Chapter 12

Janice's Healing Journey:
Saying Goodbye to Superwoman
Janice Barnwell

Have you ever met a woman who seems to have it all together? She successfully juggles her career, family, home, and community involvements seamlessly? Perhaps, you've bumped into her at your church or a community function or maybe even in your home? I have met quite a few of these women. Many of them were close relatives, like my mother and my grandmother.

These women are superwomen. A superwoman is an exceptional woman who succeeds in having a career and raising a family. (Merriam Webster) On the surface, this may look impressive to some, but invisible and often harmful consequences can result in taking on this role.

Like many women of color, I wore a cape and saved the day. A devoted mother and busy professional, I worked hard to obtain four degrees, becoming licensed as a Professional Counselor and as a Clinical Supervisor. I established a private practice and later a non- profit. I was deeply committed to my family, my clients, and my community. The only problem was that I was not as committed to caring for myself. So, when I received the results from my mammogram in 2016, it was a wake-up call.

I was diagnosed with ductile carcinoma (breast cancer). I was shocked, devastated, and a complete emotional wreck. After picking myself up from the floor, I had a vivid recall of my mother's experience. She, too, had been diagnosed with breast cancer.

Mama's Journey

My mother was affectionately called Rose by family and close friends. She was one of 15 children, born on December 12, 1916. She was my BEST friend, mentor, role model, and always expressed her unconditional love for me, even when it was probably difficult to do.

Mama was an educator, a woman of great faith and character. She was kind, gentle, and an incredibly wise woman. To know her was to love her. Mama was very grounded in who she was. She strongly believed that being educated allowed people of color to participate in the American dream. As a young child, I can recall my mother teaching many of her relatives who did not have the opportunity to go to school to receive their primary education.

After teaching students in the segregated public schools, my mother spent time in the evening teaching her adult relatives how to read and sign their names. Mama did not charge them any money; instead, they operated under the barter system. Many of our relatives lived off the land and or sea. They always provided us with an abundance of fresh vegetables, game caught from hunting, deer meat, rabbit and fresh seafood, all kinds of fish, shrimp, oysters, conch, crab, and clams.

My mother's kindness, love, and patience are why she was given an abundance of farms to table vegetables and a lot of seafood. Mama never asked of them or required them to provide us with food. Mama was a giver; she shared her abundance with others freely. Mama would always say, "when much is given, much is also required of you."

Mama would light up when she saw the excitement and pride that radiated in our relative faces as they could read and replace an X with their authentic signatures. My mother demonstrated her love for her relatives and her love of teaching and educating others. Education is a God-given right that people of color were denied during the era of slavery. It was against the law.

Mama and I spent a lot of time together as her youngest child. My Dad died during the beginning of my freshman year in college. Mama bravely assumed the role of being a single parent, being a career woman, being active in her church, being involved in community affairs, and assisting in caring for my elderly beloved grandmother. I could share many more examples of the wonderful acts of kindness shown by my mother to others, and the endless unconditional love from my dear mother.

Since her death on January 6, 1996, I think about her and her warrior spirit. If our ANCESTORS survived slavery and Jim Crow laws, we could survive the challenges faced today. Our faith in GOD and prayers are our weapons. Lastly, I recall my mother singing or humming, "May the work I've done speak for me" and "It is well with my soul." I can say so much more about my mother and the beautiful relationship we had; that would be an entire chapter and more.

Mama was diagnosed in the early spring of 1984. Mama was holding my son, Chauncey, then five months old, coming up the steps to the back door. She tripped and fell while protecting Chauncey from experiencing any injuries. By the next morning, Mama had a big hard lump in her left breast. Her primary physician encouraged her to schedule a biopsy at Beaufort Memorial Hospital in Beaufort, South Carolina. She had a radical breast removed, her left breast, seemingly endless weeks of chemotherapy.

I was overwhelmed with grief because everything happened so quickly. My mother remained calm and at peace with the diagnosis. Mama declared that Chauncey saved her life. Mama would often see the positive aspect of most situations she encountered. My mother demonstrated extraordinary faith, peace, and a calm about her that I quickly emulated. Mama declared that it was not a death sentence. I never saw my mother with any illness. She never took a sick day off from work; she never stayed in her bed past 8:00 am. I never saw her openly grieve the death of Daddy. What I always saw was SUPERWOMAN in action. I did not realize how much of my mother's lifestyle I had adopted and incorporated into my lifestyle.

My Diagnosis

Clearly, I was in denial of how much I was becoming my mother. I never imagined that I would receive the diagnosis of having breast cancer one day in my future. Ironically, like my mother, my left breast was where the ductile carcinoma was identified. I was so busy BEING SUPERWOMAN, as that is what I saw all my life from Mama, my grandmother, and many other women of color that it was my norm. I was not mindful of how devasting it could be as it relates to my health. I felt guilty and unproductive if I was not fully engaged in multiple projects.

After having many days and nights of UGLY cries and pleading to God to heal my body, I slowly began to put my BIG girl panties on. I took the first step by reaching out to other cancer survivors who freely shared with me. It became a WAKE-UP CALL to change my lifestyle, disrupt old patterns that were of no use. I diligently began to research and better understand my body. Mary Ellen Barton was one of my role models and teachers. I read books, listened to tapes, and watched videos to learn about the benefits of eating a plant-based diet, the benefits of juicing and forgiving myself for putting unhealthy food and being around toxic unloving, and unkind people.

I did my due diligence before scheduling a date for surgery. In addition to my son, Chauncey, who never left my side, I was blessed to have a supportive community of sister-friends who were dedicated, caring women of integrity: Andrea Ussery Sweeney, Roberle Collier Pratt, Sharon Alexander, Pat Martin, Catherine Young, Glenda Murray-Farris,

128

Frances Slaughter, Cynthia Williams, and Wilhelmenia Jeter Mathias.

These women did not allow the distance to interfere with being mighty prayer warriors. They surrounded me with love, light, and healing energy, which helped ease my fear and anxiety. Incorporating the proper diet, rest, exercise, and surrounding myself with loving, positive people helped speed up the healing process.

To date, I am THANKFUL to say; medical reports reveal that my body is cancer-free!

Closing Thoughts

Experiencing a crisis often creates an opportunity for a radical lifestyle change. After being diagnosed with cancer, I began to view life from a different lens. Like the carnation, I am from a culture that is filled with pride and beauty. We are the Gullah people. Strong, spiritual, resilient, and powerful. All of this, I am and will continue to be. I just needed to step back and learn to include my wellbeing in the equation of serving others. I am not superwoman, and neither are you. Our bodies break down when we do not take care of ourselves.

I encourage you to have your yearly mammogram. I was fortunate that when I was diagnosed, the cancer was caught early on in stage one. Just because you are healthy or doing important life work, these are not reasons to ignore prioritizing this important responsibility. If you do not have insurance, you can contact the National Cancer Institute (1-800-4-CANCER) or the American Cancer Society (1-800-ACS-2345) for a free mammogram.

I leave you with these simple reminders: Love yourself. Forgive easily. Let go of the past. Stay away from toxic people. Stay connected to your faith. Ask for help. Say no more often. If you see yourself in my story, the sooner you can lay superwoman to rest, the better. Place her in the archives where she belongs and start down the path of a more healthy, balanced, and whole life where you can live a beautiful life in full bloom.

My name is Janice Barnwell, and I will continue to BLOOM wherever I am planted.

Meet Janice Barnwell

Janice is a fifth generation native of Hilton Head Island, South Carolina. She is the youngest of three children born to the late Edward and Rosalie White Barnwell.

Janice has 41 years of experience in the field of human services. She obtained her master's degree in Clinical Counseling from Webster University, St. Louis, MO. Prior to becoming a Licensed Professional Counselor and a Licensed Professional Counselor Supervisor, Janice obtained a Master's degree in Addiction Counseling and a bachelor's degree in Social Work from Benedict College in Columbia, SC.

In 2006 Janice established Barnwell Counseling, LLC, located in Bluffton, SC. She has maintained her private practice since 2001. Presently, she works part-time providing telehealth counseling to individuals and couples.

Janice continued to enhance her skills by becoming a Certified Life Coach in 2009, when she began seeing clients who were changing careers and re-entering the workforce. She is trained as a facilitator for Pattern Changing for Abused Women. She has offered several workshops in the Hilton Head Island/Bluffton area. Janice also has extensive training in the field of trauma.

Janice is the mother of a son Chauncey, and a grandmother of a one-year old granddaughter, Clara.

Email: healinghaven01@gmail.com
Phone: 843.422.1206

KRISTINA ARMSTRONG

An African Violet represents gratitude, appreciation, and recognition.

The African Violet has special meaning to me because both my maternal great grandmother Eleanor and my maternal grandmother Hazel grew them.

I promise myself to colorfully bloom like the African Violet. To continue to welcome life, reimagined opportunities and possibilities to fill the pages of my journals and future writings. To keep learning and sharing positive and uplifting life empowering information.

Chapter 13

Good Steps
Kristina Griffin Armstrong

"There are three things you need to leave behind: your photographs, your library and your personal journals."

Excerpts from The Treasury of Quotes by Jim Rohn. The Master of Success 1993 by Jim Rohn International.

I listened intently and wrote quickly as Mr. Rohn continued to explain. He said that if no one ever knew us, they could learn something about the life we led by looking at our photographs, reading our books, and journals. These three things would reveal what people, places, and things influenced and motivated us. To this day, Mr. Rohn's seminar left a lasting and powerful impression on me because I am a collector of all three.

I have countless photos of every area of my life: childhood, family, friends, college, career, business. Plus, treasured photos of my ancestors. They are special documented moments in time. I remember using the Kodak instamatic cameras with the square flash, then the others with the instant picture you would shake and blow for the picture to appear. Later the Canon Power shot, my stepfather gave me, which unfortunately was misplaced. Thankfully, I purchased a similar one with his help.

Photos and videos of family, friends, and coworkers are now taken with my smart phone. I'm not surprised to hear at family celebrations and special events someone say, "Please no more photos." However, in the last few years, photos and videos are mostly reserved for the adorable poses and smiling faces of my two youngest nieces, Bria and Angel. They too let me know when they have had enough. Another joy I have is taking photos of nature, flowers, and landscapes.

Since the age of twelve, I have outlined life changing events and special moments I experienced. Often, because I was unhappy, sad or fearful and needed clarity and support. Other times, because I was happy, excited, and planning the next goal to achieve. The process was simple. I identified the life events which corresponded to the specific age or age range at the time. Like, moving to Los Angeles ages 8-12. Living and studying in Mexico from ages 12-17. Seeing these events outlined on paper made it more real and meaningful. It was documentation of a unique and special life which belonged to me. Whether happy or sad I claimed them all, they were part of me. I took time to reflect and look at the lessons learned and reasons why I had made certain choices and decisions.

I noticed the patterns and differences in these events. The peaks and valleys the ups and downs. In a way they provided direction and guidance. But what I noticed most was my constant moving forward against the obstacles, achieving goals, learning, sharing, growing, changing, and blooming along the way. I continue this process today.

Being a truth seeker and a truth teller, I seek knowledge and I share it. Providing information, education, and guidance to help others make informed decisions to improve their lives is my mission. Or to quote my husband Mark, *"This is how I serve the universe."* I know for sure I did not get here by accident. I arrived here on purpose, guided, and directed by early and continuous exposure through the years of personal development/achievement, success, educational tools, and resources.

I love books. I collect and read various types of books. As a child my mother, Ramona, was my earliest teacher and influence. She provided me with books, diaries, and journals to learn reading and writing skills. I still have one of the books she gave me at age 8. Happiness is Everywhere by Dean Walley. It was my first personal development book.

Another important influence years later was my involvement as a founding member of The People's Network (TPN) a personal development company created in the early 90's. I was reading books and listening to tapes by great, influential motivational speakers, teachers, and trainers, like Les Brown, Jim Rohn, Mark Victor Hansen, Brian Tracy, and many others. They were primarily known to the fortune 500 companies, but now were accessible to everyone.

I was fortunate to meet many of these great minds. Attend their trainings, workshops to learn and better my own life. I facilitated and coordinated meetings to spread the good news about TPN to anyone who wanted information to improve their self, career, relationships, finances, health, etc. Sharing life changing information with others has been a major theme in my life.

The first sixty years of my life journey have involved taking many Good Steps. Learning, growing, and discovering myself has been a choice, and not an accident. I have always wanted to be my best self and manifest all the good I can in this lifetime. But at times I have let issues in the past, fear of the unknown and faith in my capabilities keep me from taking the next good step.

Good Step Principles.

I share the following list of what I have learned along my journey. They remind me of who I am and what I'm here to do. Each of these good steps bloomed one by one from my experiences described above.

1. **The Serenity Prayer:** This is one of my mothers' favorite prayers. "God grant me the serenity to accept the things I cannot change, courage to change the things I can and the wisdom to know the difference." In 2011, I

137

was unhappy and depressed with my life. I examined my life and wrote down all the things I needed to accept, what I needed to change and the difference between the two. This was the most difficult. In the end it provided me with clarity, peace, and purpose.

2. **How does it get better than this?** Asking this question, manifests every day, in every way, in small and big ways. Unexpected answers to questions, information and resources appear from people, places, and things. You just keep asking the question and be open to receiving good. Accepting the good and being thankful for the good.

3. **Denials & Affirmations:** My first affirmation was I am healthy, happy and whole. Through the years I learned how important it is to also deny or reject what I don't want in my life and also claim what I do want in my life. It's important we speak the truth of who we are or want to be.

4. **Be thankful, appreciative & grateful:** Upon wakening in the morning I say Thank you God for all good things. See the good, hear the good and speak good. Nothing is too small or too big. It's all good. Be thankful and appreciative for the good that manifests in so different ways. Take nothing for granted.

5. **Be your biggest fan & loudest cheerleader:** The support is there and willing to help, but you and the spirit within ultimately are your biggest supporter. Only you can decide if you want to move forward, do the work, and change. This requires courage and trust. Release the ego. Let go. Trust self and look within. It's a slow process. With God guiding, directing, and protecting you, you are never alone.

6. **Self-Love and Control:** We create our own happiness. Others can add to our happiness and share in it. No one can complete us. As a people pleaser, I had to learn that even though loving others was not received or reciprocated, I had to respect and love myself for the

138

good I wanted to share. Once I realized this, I felt a sense of release and relief and did not have to put energy into trying to control people, situations, and circumstances.

7. **Time will promote you or expose you:** We all will live a certain amount of time on this earth. How will we use this time? It's our choice. We must decide if we will face our fears, forgive, let go of the past and trust the process of life by learning, growing and changing. What mark will you leave?

8. **Half a dozen things**. In anything you want to achieve in life you generally only have to do about 6 or 7 general activities to reach your goal. Not 15, 20 or 30. Just a few general activities consistently over time.

9. **What do you need to do more of or less of?** You can apply this question to any goal you want to achieve in your personal or professional life. If we want something to change, to be better or different, ask this question. What activities, ways of thinking, behavior do I need to do more of or less of to achieve my goal?

10. **Always acknowledge the Good.** Its' always there no matter how small or big. Its' a powerful guiding force in our life. We just need to be observant. I always try and find the good in everything. Even in challenging situations. Maybe it's not visible at that moment. But I always see good manifest at some point.

The Good Step Principles are ever present and useful in my daily life and work. The importance of balance, harmony and health in my body, mind, and spirit. My desire to manifest all the good I can in this lifetime and be more of service to others.

I mentioned earlier I enjoy taking photos of flowers, nature, and landscapes. I love all different types of flowers, but my favorite is the African Violet. It has special meaning to me because both my maternal great grandmother Eleanor and my maternal grandmother Hazel grew them. I see them now blossoming in an array of shapes and colors displayed on their sunlit kitchen windowsills. I too have grown them over the years sometimes successfully and sometimes not.

I promise myself to colorfully bloom like the African Violet. To continue to welcome life reimagined, opportunities, and possibilities to fill the pages of my journals and future writings. To keep learning and sharing positive and uplifting life-empowering information. To read the books that teach, educate, inspire, and enlighten me. To continue to take beloved photos of family, friends, and the things I love which nourish my heart and replenish my soul. To be a committed, lifelong learner, knowledge seeker and knowledge giver. To be of service to my community to stop injustice, police brutality and promote peace and equality.

It is my hope this chapter will be useful to you and will motivate you to choose at least one skill or Good Step Principle to better any area of your life. That it will give you more knowledge and information and validate what you already know to be true. Most of this is not new information. It has been paid forward, edited, expanded, and shared over several lifetimes. What is important is how it affects you and how you and others can use it to manifest more of the good you want in our own life.

I encourage you to promise yourself to keep improving the life you have or create the life you want and desire. Begin as I did by first taking an honest, and truthful inventory of where you are right now in your life. In this present moment, here and now. Are you happy, sad, fearful, hopeful, excited, worried, confident, uncertain?

Now, repeat calmly this simple question. How does it get better than this? Expect to receive answers. All journeys begin one good step at a time. Enjoy!

My name is Kristina Griffin Armstrong, and I will continue to BLOOM wherever I am planted.

Meet Kristina Griffin Armstrong

Kristina believes sharing life changing information, and skills empowers others to make better informed decisions; promotes personal development and lifelong learning.

Kristina is a certified career services professional & career development coach with experience and training in program management, training, and coaching. Specifically, in career services, addiction prevention/recovery management, instructional design, and development.

She has a BA in Spanish from the University of California – Santa Barbara and lived and studied five years in Jocotepec, Jalisco, Mexico.

She is the owner of Good Steps Training & Coaching, LLC. and provides nonprofit consultation services. Kristina worked eleven years with Goodwill of North Georgia participating in the initial growth and planning of several career centers and managing the *first bilingual career center* in a Goodwill store.

Kristina is a member of the National Career Development Association and board member with the Georgia Career Development Association. She also Volunteers with the AARP Georgia State office.

Email: goodstepstc1@gmail.com
Phone: 770 403-88

LATRICIA SCRIVEN

The magnolia is a symbol of poise, pride, and perseverance; and the strength of its bloom exemplifies self-respect and self-esteem.

The magnolia is both my state flower and a beautiful representation of my life and journey. This alluring blossom is so fragrant, it can fill the air with its powerful scent. I image that, if personified, this living creation that is the magnolia would neither apologize for its bold presence nor try to hide its captivating aroma. I certainly did not begin my journey this way, but somewhere along the way, "I found God in myself and I loved her fiercely!"

143

Chapter 14

The Power of *AND*
Latricia Edwards Scriven

I am Latricia Darlene Edwards Scriven. I own every part of my name because each part bears witness to its own power and pain. Yes, power and pain; laughter and lament. I am jovial, jazzy, and jaded; magnificent, melancholy, marvelous, and sometimes morose. As I embraced the gloriously complex dynamism of living in the spectrum, I danced a new dance free from binaries and false dichotomies. And like a fragrant magnolia dangling betwixt the thick and shiny leaves of an opulent tree... that's when I started to BLOOM!

I'm a Louisiana girl by birth. The magnolia is my state flower. I don't have "hot sauce in my bag," but I've got a lotta swag. I was born with it. It just took me a while to know it. I know it now, and I don't only know it, I own it, I dance in it, I breathe it, I live it! I've learned that to be fully and authentically me – beautifully blemished and perfectly imperfect – is a holy act of worship that honors the One from whom my very essence flows. Quoted by Nelson Mandela, Marianne Williamson said it like this: "We ask ourselves, who am I to be brilliant, gorgeous, talented and fabulous? Actually, who are you not to be? You are a child of God."

It's beautiful to know who you are – to really know – and to love all that is you. Today I know and love this ever evolving me in ways that have changed my life forever. And it wasn't always this way. Let's go back.

Chapel Cap Baptist

"Either you're going to submit or be my equal." That's what he said to me before adding, "You can't have it both ways."

I didn't realize it at the time, but this was the conundrum that I'd faced much of my life and one that would continue beyond that moment. It took years for me to break free of the embedded, ingrained, and reinforced system that tried to squeeze the life from my soul.

"Why do we need to wear chapel caps when we take communion?" I was young when I asked, though I don't recall exactly how young. It was a Saturday morning, and we were in choir rehearsal. I was in the cherubim choir, and we were practicing with the adults that day. I didn't want to be defiant; I just really wanted to understand.

I didn't know what the little white circular doily on my head meant and why I had to wear it. I just knew that I better have one! No one had ever taken the time to explain to me why I couldn't eat at the table of our Lord if I didn't have a chapel cap (or at least a white napkin) on my head. And why did only the women and girls wear them? I had an inquiring mind, and it wanted to know.

"We honor God when we cover our heads," I recall her saying. "Because it's in the bible," declared one of the few men who spoke. "If you don't have on a chapel cap, then you can't take communion. It's required, and that's it," announced another.

Looking back on it, they were probably a lot more frustrated with my curiosity than I understood at the time. With brows raised, head tilted, and shoulders slightly shrugged, I kept going, "so why don't the boys wear them? Why just the girls? What happens if I don't have one?"

After one or two more rounds of playing "why," someone beckoned the pastor to the choir stand to settle the matter once and for all. Pastor was cool instead of bothered as he flipped the worn pages of the only version that mattered to

1 Corinthians 11. His deep voice reverberated through the air. *"But I would have you know that the head of every man is Christ, and the head of the woman is the man, and the head of Christ is God."* After continuing about a wife dishonoring her husband if she prayed or prophesied with her head uncovered, he took a breath. Possibly hearing the thoughts sprinting through my cranium, he paused.

Pastor's eyes were in my direction, but his words hit us all. "You've asked good questions Little Edwards, and I'm going to be honest. Sometimes we do things out of tradition. In the Baptist church, it is a tradition for women and girls to wear chapel caps during communion." He talked about how the tradition related to scripture then shared, "wearing a chapel cap is not a requirement of scripture, and I am okay if anyone chooses not to wear one when participating in the Lord's Supper."

A lump moved down my throat as my pupils bounced from face to face. Furrowed foreheads and pursed lips filled the room as the side conversations commenced. And that was the end of that. My face relaxed, and my pearly whites began to show. My chapel cap days were over.

I grew into young adulthood, moved to the Midwest for grad school, got married, and began my own family. By the time we returned to Chapel Cap Baptist Church, women were allowed to pray, preach, and even acknowledge a call to ministry. BUT they were not allowed to sit in the pulpit, a place still reserved for men. Another decade passed, and I was back at CCBC attending a family member's funeral. To my delight, a woman stood proudly behind the sacred desk to give the eulogy. My heart was strangely warmed.

Weaker Vessel Apostolic

"Sis. Scriven, as a woman, you are the 'weaker vessel.' Accept it." Perhaps, the statement wouldn't have caught me so off guard had it come from a man. But it didn't. A church sister-friend said it to me as she proudly embraced her

147

divinely sanctioned place in the universe and urged me to accept mine.

I was a newlywed, and we had not been in the area very long. We were in a small town in the Midwest that boasted two historically black colleges (the two were one before they split and formed a public side and a private side) and a seminary. Darryl and I were both assistant professors at the private HBCU. But it all started at Fulmer's Grocery. Darryl was at the local market when he met a gentleman who invited us to attend his church. So, we went.

It was a small apostolic church that didn't just reinforce the chapel cap message, it took it to whole new levels. Not only were women not allowed in the pulpit, but we were considered to be unclean when we were on our cycles. Yes, you heard me – unclean – Leviticus style! And there's more. For women, jewelry was worldly, "painted" faces were sinful, pants could only be worn by guys, and it was an act of harlotry to cut your hair.

Smothered by the dark cloud of a socially constructed system that held captive both women and men, I would sometimes cry on Sunday mornings because I did not want to go to church. In Weaker Vessel Apostolic, I felt oppressed in ways that I could not fully articulate. And, while I was sure that my husband would be pained if he knew the depths of my struggle, it took years before I let him in. I shared bits and pieces along the way, but I wasn't sure that he would understand the way I needed him to. How could he?

Now, let me be clear. It wasn't all bad. I met great, praying people who loved to laugh and who were committed to God "in a very special way" (LOL, that's an inside joke and there's no time to explain). We celebrated love feasts, our families got together frequently, and the ladies enjoyed all night prayer while the men went all-day fishing. We joked, we played, we shared life together.

And it was all fun and games 'til I started walking around looking "homely." Yep, homely. That's how Dr. V described it. Dr. V was an administrator at the university where I worked. She watched my transformation as I spiraled into a different version of myself. Dr. V jumped straight into concerned mama mode when she called me into her office. "Girl, what is happening to you? I am going to call your mother and tell her how you're looking because I know she does not know that you're walking around looking homely like this! You had so much style when you came. What happened?"

I still wonder to this day; did I really look that bad? Come on now, homely? I'm pretty sure she was exaggerating, right? The worst part of attending Weaker Vessel Apostolic was that I did it to myself. I moved from feeling smothered, oppressed, and devalued as a woman to pulling out the chapel cap and tossing it on my own head. I could have resisted. I could have rebelled. I could have simply stood my ground while bringing unintended "shame to my husband" – because shame on him to have a less than a subservient wife. One of the brothers actually said that to me. Shame.

Instead, I gave in to the culture and spiritualized mandates because they had become my family and I did not want to do anything that would cause my siblings to stumble. I thought it was the right thing to do. No, I didn't believe that women shouldn't wear pants, or jewelry, or makeup, or colorful garments, or whatever else they said we shouldn't wear or do to escape damnation. But Paul had my mind. "If food makes my brother stumble, I will never eat meat, lest I make my brother stumble." Paul's words insinuated that the least I could do was not to cause them to stumble. So, I didn't. I adjusted my invisible chapel cap and kept it moving.

Everything changed when Destini arrived. Destini was our firstborn, and I didn't want her to grow up in the vice-grip that pervaded Weaker Vessel Church. I needed her to be free.

"I will not allow our daughter to grow up in this." With drops of water forming just beneath my eyelids, I raised my voice in anger and exasperation as I spoke. Darryl tilted his

149

head in anticipation of what might come next. I wasn't angry at him, or the church, or at being called homely. I was angry at myself for becoming this new iteration of myself. When I look back on it, Weaker Vessel Apostolic was a significant part of my journey of becoming, and it took a long time before I could remember those days without a rush of pain and resentment.

Pastor P

I found Pastor P. in Louisiana. The P is for Phenomenal. She was a woman. Phenomenally. A phenomenal pastor woman, that's Pastor P.

I loved the community feel of the Pentecostal, non-denominational church that she pastored. We were an intimate, close-knit crew, and everybody seemed to want more of Jesus. We didn't have musicians, but the way those worshippers sang to the background rhythms of a track made us forget that there was such a thing as a keyboard. Women, men, children, youth – we were all present, accounted for, and making every effort to present our best to God.

Along with Pastor P, there were apostles, teachers, prophets, and evangelists among us. "We believe in the five-fold ministry." That's what Pastor P would say. "Everything we need is right here in the house. We just need to pump the well to get it out. Y'all better 'stir up' those gifts!"

It was in this church that I found a glimpse of a new kind of freedom. I prayed, preached, sang, evangelized, and taught. I stirred up the gifts and pumped the well for more. My hubby did, too. We learned, we grew, and we served. Together. It was a joyful time.

As a layer of foundations, Pastor P's husband identified with the office of apostle, and she was the pastor. It was clear that Pastor Phenomenal was the shepherd of Five-Fold Non-Denominational Church. It was also clear that her husband was the head of their household. You can't always run and hide from one-way submission. Even as a pastor, Madame

Phenomenal could not escape the hierarchy. It was meant to be that way. I was back in that Saturday rehearsal at Chapel Cap Baptist, "I want you to understand that the head of every man is Christ, the head of a wife is her husband."

That's why when my cousin announced that she was a pastor many years before my experience with Pastor P, I couldn't embrace it at the time. Perhaps she called herself a pastor; but surely that could not be. Back then, I wondered how my cousin could've missed 1 Timothy 2, "I do not permit a woman to teach or to exercise authority over a man; rather, she is to remain quiet."

Submit or be equal; it can't be both. Maybe I was the one who missed it. Perhaps, like Pastor P, I could have authority in the church as long as I understood my proper place at home.

My buds were starting to show. I could smell a bit of the magnolia fragrance wafting through the air when we were with Pastor P and Five-Fold. It was too early to tell the magnitude of what was growing, but I knew enough to know that "eyes had not seen, and ears had not heard" the things that God was preparing. Who knew that this kind of fierce love for the divinity that existed in me and as me would ever be possible? God knew, and the Spirit was working in me to discern.

New Soil

Years passed. Now, with three children, one husband, and having experienced much sunshine, rain, fertilizer, and care, it was time for new soil. Off to Atlanta, we went. We moved to the outskirts of Atlanta to the city of Alpharetta. There are sooooo many stories I could tell about our time in Alpharetta. This is where our children grew up; it's where our marriage grew up; it's where I grew up. It's where... hmmm, maybe I should have subtitled this Growing Up.

For me, one thing has remained constant during the stages of growth. Laughter! Everyone who knows me knows that I LOVE to laugh. It's my superpower. Most times, I laugh because my brain thinks something is funny. Other times, I laugh because my emotions get mixed up. I should be crying, but I'm cackling like a hyena on the Lion King. And then, there are those times that I laugh to keep from punching somebody in the throat. I mean, not that I would ever punch anyone (wink). Yes, there was that one time I flipped over a table, but didn't Jesus do that, too? So rather than punch or flip tables, I laugh! You know that laugh. The one that says, "I know you ain't 'bout to try me?!" That one. Hubby says I have a little gangsta in me that no one can see coming until it's too late! LOL!

I'm saying, just because I'm talking about blooming doesn't mean that life has been all flowers! Fertilizer has had its place.

I Was Missing Something

I don't recall the exact moment that it happened. I only know that it did. There was a moment in my life where I received – unapologetically, without shame, and as unto the Lord – that I am enough. And not just enough; I am more than enough. I am created in the image of the Divine, beautifully, and wondrously made, and God called me Good before I was called anything else.

I was missing what was inside me all along, waiting to be discovered. When I embraced and loved the truth of all that is me, I experienced liberation in a new way. I knew the Truth, and I became free. And not only did I become free, but I also continue to walk into new levels of freedom every day. I was free to love myself wholly and without boundaries. I was free to discover all that God had designed me to be. I was free from the perspectives and perceptions of others. I was free from internalized limitations and lies. I was free from dimming my light so that others wouldn't be blinded by it. I was free!

As I said before, it's beautiful to know who you are – to really know – and to love all that is you. And when we can really know ourselves – the fabulous and the flaws – and love ourselves anyway? Well, that's when we know we've tapped into that agape' kinda love; the kind of love that compels us to love our neighbors as ourselves. "I found God in myself, and I loved her fiercely!"

What do you love, and I mean absolutely LOVE about yourself? Take your time. Think about it. Say it out loud. We'll wait.

It is a travesty that many of us are not accustomed to complimenting ourselves regularly. It's as if we fear that to say what we love about ourselves will be conceived as vain, as conceited, as prideful, as unacceptable. And far worse, we have so little practice with self-affirmations that some of us find ourselves at a loss for words and unworthy of our own admiration and love.

What do I love about me? I love my smile and my imperfect teeth that come along with it. I love that I love to laugh, and I love that I "play too much." (Is there a such thing as playing too much?) I love that I'm witty with a sprinkle of country, holy with a dash of hood, and realistically optimistic with a pinch of petty. I love that I love corny math jokes, twirling in the grass for no reason and that I'm beginning to show signs of aging even though I try to color some of the signs away.

I love my locs! My hair has been a part of my love journey and my journey with my daughters. Right now, I'm wearing them much shorter than usual. I woke up one day and just felt like cutting my hair, so I called up my stylist. It wasn't cut very evenly (don't tell her I told you). Short parts and shorter parts randomly layer my scalp. And I love it. It's perfectly imperfect, just like me!!

Now your turn to practice again. In the mirror this time. What do you LOVE about you? Self-love is a gamechanger!

A New Leaf On Life

Let the blooming begin. The seedling had germinated, buds were bursting forth, I had a new leaf on life! The tiny young bud of a majestic magnolia was beginning to open itself to the fullness of life as it offered its aroma as a gift to the world.

It wasn't that I had low self-esteem growing up. I didn't. It wasn't that I lacked confidence. I had it. It was that before I was old enough to know what it was, I was fighting it. I was wrestling with an intangible, insidious, and sometimes invisible gender-biased system that prescribed roles based on anatomy and physiology while consciously and subconsciously reinforcing antiquated notions of womanhood as it elevated maleness to godliness.

After living in Alpharetta for several years and serving as a faculty member and department chairperson at a university nearby, I was off to seminary. I didn't go because I had dreams of being like Pastor P. Far from it. I went because I wanted to explore theological questions and concepts in ways that wouldn't get me kicked out of Sunday school. I had questions that needed answers, and what I found was so much more.

As my theology changed, I changed. I re-discovered women who I thought I'd known. I was encountering them through new lenses and had a voracious appetite for more. By now, I had already found God in myself via *For Colored Girls* and had begun a journey of reinterpretation as I read Merlin Stone's *When God Was a Woman* and watched as she exorcised evil from Eve. I loved reading *The Shack* and relating to God as the black woman I needed her to be. And now, at the Interdenominational Theological Center by way of Gammon Theological Seminary, I was encountering the unsung strength of Jezebel, the fearless audacity of Esther, the transcendent wisdom of Deborah, the strategic brilliance of Naomi, the unprecedented bravery of Mary, the abundant wealth of Lydia, and the unrelenting boldness of the

154

Daughters of Zelophehad. As I re-encountered these women, I re-encountered myself. And I BLOOMED!

The Power of And

"Either you're going to submit or be my equal. You can't have it both ways." It was my husband who said it. He said it while we were attending Weaker Vessel Apostolic. Even then, he was advocating for egalitarianism. And though he was combating his remnants of patriarchy, he was letting me know that I was his equal. He was telling me that no matter what anyone else thought or said, there would be no hierarchies with us. Our lives were intricately and inextricably connected. We led our household together; we made decisions together; we co-created our lives together. He would always say that we both had drum-major instincts. I would say that "iron sharpens iron."

The truth is that it wasn't submission or equality; it was submission and equality. It wasn't either; it wasn't or. It is both; and it is and. What I learned was that there is power in submission and power in equality. We both submitted one to another as equals. The power is in the and. This insight wasn't just a powerful catalyst that allowed us to unlock buried treasures about relationships and marriage. *And* is a powerful key to the kin-dom of self-discovery and abundant love that holds it all together. This three-letter connective conjunction allowed all the complex parts of me to join together to create a new whole.

Sometimes, we try to separate ourselves into pieces – the pieces we want to keep and the pieces we don't; the parts that are healed, and the parts in need of healing; the bits we call good and the bits we call bad. The problem is that this way of existing keeps us disconnected from ourselves and others. It prevents us from being whole and embracing all the pieces as sacred.

We often speak of loving One who was fully human and fully divine. The One who was filled with compassion, grace, wisdom, and forgiveness was the same One who got angry, flipped tables, needed time away from taking care of everyone, and sometimes had a smart mouth. Fully human and fully divine. There was power and purpose in the and for Jesus, and the same is true for us.

"Just because it's simple, don't mean it's easy." I do not recall who I heard say it first, but I have repeated it often. It's simple, but it ain't easy! It's simple to be you, and it is not always easy. Sis! Be fully and authentically you – beautifully blemished and perfectly imperfect – as a holy act of worship that honors the God from whom your very essence flows. You are much more than you think you are. Own it, dance in it, breathe it, live it! Find God in yourself and love her fiercely.

As a mathematician, I wish I had a step-by-step formula to tell you exactly what to do. I don't. What I can say is trust the process. And when you can't trust the process, create the process. We are co-creators with a benevolent God who loves us with an everlasting love. She's rooting for us!

My name is Latricia Edwards Scriven, and I will continue to BLOOM wherever I am planted.

Meet Latricia Scriven

Rev. Dr. Latricia Scriven is the Pastor of New Life United Methodist Church in Tallahassee, FL, and Pastor/Director of the IMPACT@FAMU Wesley Foundation at Florida A&M University. Pastor Scriven absolutely loves being called to ministry! She is passionate about empowering women, strengthening marriages, and supporting marginalized and vulnerable populations.

Latricia has an undergraduate degree in Mathematics, as well as master's and Ph.D. degrees from Purdue University in Mathematics Education and Educational Administration, respectively. Dr. Scriven also earned a Master of Divinity degree from Gammon Theological Seminary in Atlanta, GA. She has held faculty positions in universities across the country and is currently an Adjunct Professor of Religion at Florida A&M University in Tallahassee.

Latricia is married to her phenomenal husband, Dr. Darryl Scriven, and they have three wonderfully talented children. Latricia loves traveling the world, playing Uno and Sorry with her family, sharing life with her students and congregation, and laughing uncontrollably with friends.

Website: https://www.newlifeumctally.org/
Telephone: (850) 877-4823

LILLIAN BROWNING

*A sunflower represents pure thoughts,
adoration, and dedication.*

*I have chosen the Sunflower as a representation of
my inner spirit. Many years ago, I was made aware
that the Sunflower follows the Sun as it passes
across the sky. This is where the Sunflower touched
my spirit. In-spite of all the difficulties life brings;
the Sunflower follows the Sun. It has inspired me
to follow the Sun / Son.*

Chapter 15

The Kiss I Missed
Lillian Leticia Browning

I will begin my story at the time when my life journey significantly began. I didn't realize how much growth can come from so much pain. So. I begin:

He left for work without kissing me good-bye that morning. I cried; I knew something had changed. I knew at that moment; my world would never be the same. I knew my marriage was over. My thoughts turned immediately to my children. I wanted so much for them to have both parents, but how?

You see, due to a traumatic teen-life, I made a poor choice and became pregnant at 17 years old. My boyfriend, who later became my husband, was a good guy. He was well-raised. He was a protector and provider for our little family. I was truly blessed that he was the father of my child. Within 18 months of our daughters' birth, I gave birth to our son. My then-husband worked hard and provided us with all the necessities and emotional support our young family needed. However, due to my traumatic past, I didn't know how to value his actions.

A look into life before my relationship and marriage reveals abuse, mostly physical, but some mental. Beginning at the age of 13, I experienced weekly beatings from my step-grandfather (now deceased). He was a functioning alcoholic. As I look back, the beatings were his warped way of keeping me under control, while at the same time fighting his demons.

At 16 years old, my step-grandfather finally allowed me to see my mother in Los Angeles, Ca. I was born in Los Angeles and sent to my paternal grandmother and step-grandfather at 11 months of age. I was told that the goal was to allow my parents to work without having me stay the week at a babysitter, only returning to my parents on weekends. No one knew it was to be a one-way journey.

Due to my parents' divorce, a few years after I arrived in Louisiana, my paternal grandparents refused to send me back to Los Angeles, even though my mother had legal custody of me. My father returned to Louisiana. My mother, being a Panamanian immigrant, was told that she could not legally have me return as long as my father was with me. We will never know whether that legal advice was correct.

My time with my mother was lanced with major emotions and drama. The beauty there was that I met my half-siblings (I was my father's only child). My oldest sister became my greatest ally. In the years that followed, she became my greatest mentor, nurturer, and role model.

My desire to return to live with my grandparents hurt and confused my mother. She was angry and would lash out verbally, but she did not stop me from leaving. Upon my return, the beatings stopped; however, I was now more confused and alone than I had ever felt in my life.

So, back to that morning when there was no kiss goodbye. During those years of marriage, unbeknownst to myself, I had become the very thing I was attempting to escape, I became abusive. Verbally and sometimes physically, I lashed out. So, on this day, the buck stopped here, as evidenced by the missing kiss good-bye. My husband had found solace in someone else and started a family before our divorce. I don't think he stopped loving me; he simply stopped tolerating me.

As I traversed those painful days, I could not escape knowing the role I had played in creating this reality. I tried with every fiber of my being to make things right. But I was unsuccessful. Too much had occurred in those twelve years of marriage, too much.

So, when I finally accepted that my marriage could not be fixed or saved, I stood in my living room with my arms outstretched to God and prayed. I prayed that he would not allow me or my children to slip into poverty. I prayed that my children would somehow still have their father in their lives. I asked that I become a better person. I asked that He allow me to survive this pain and thrive. I promised I would devote myself to helping other women survive and thrive if allowed me to survive. As I prayed, my spirit felt the words "With God all things are possible" (Matthew 19:26).

So, like the Sunflower, I looked up toward the Sun/Son; and began my new journey. My prayers began being answered with a swiftness. My children were blessed with a father who continued to father them. I did not sink into poverty.

Within a few years, I graduated as a Women's Healthcare Nurse Practitioner. By His grace, I was the first Nurse Practitioner to practice in my city. It was a challenging but rewarding experience. I chose to provide care for the whole woman, not only their bodies but also their spirits. Using everything that life had taught me up to that point, I provided compassionate care to every soul God divinely sent me. I began to bloom into the woman God intended me to be.

As the years passed, I saw another need in my community. Diabetes was ravaging so many. Though I had never been interested in providing diabetes care, my spirit was compelled to do so. I went to the CEO of our medical facility and asked if I could provide Diabetes Education to patients. I was given the green light to do so.

For ten years, I instructed patients on the basics of Diabetes care. The CEO then requested that I develop the diabetes program more. I asked for additional training. My first goal was to do an online program. Through divine intervention, I was accepted to a comprehensive diabetes management program at The Mayo Clinic in Rochester,

Minnesota. This was a residential program for 30 days. At one point, the program was so challenging, I cried out in the night to God, "Lord, why am I here? I don't have enough prior training to be in such an intensive program."

When I woke in the morning, my bible verse for the day was Jeremiah 29:11 "For I know the plans I have for you." I had never seen or heard that verse before. I took it as a personal message to me and continued forward in my studies. After my studies, I became a Certified Diabetes Educator, only one of three in my community.

From the day the verse was given to me, it became my mantra through all the challenges I have faced. I realized that indeed, He had plans for me to prosper me (as I had asked) and give me a fruitful future.

Many times, along my life journey, I wanted to leave the community I had been raised in. Each time there was a compelling reason that caused me to stay. I realize now that He wanted me to bloom where I was planted. He wanted me to sow seeds of compassion, and His love for each soul he brought to me. Because I recognized my imperfections, I was able to truly see the spirit of those brought before me without judging them. They could feel the unconditional acceptance and be able to get or feel healthier.

I have shared my story to let others know that God waters your prayers. He guides you to where you are to bloom. He causes you to reap the harvest of your good works. He indeed forgives all of your shortcomings and allows you to grow from the experiences.

I say to each of you, be like the Sunflower; always look up and follow the Sun/Son. Consider this; Blooming is a process. As long as we live, we grow, if we choose to.

My name is Lillian Leticia Browning, and I will continue to BLOOM wherever I am planted.

MARCHELL COLEMAN

*A Peace Lily represents calming, healing,
peace, wholeness and prosperity.*

*The peace lily is associated in Christianity with the
Virgin Mary and the Easter season. It also symbolizes
the resurrection of Jesus Christ from the dead. The
plant is from the genus Spathiphyllum, which is a
Latin word that means "peace and prosperity." Peace
lilies are known as the bringers of peace.*

*The Peace Lily principle offers hope and healing
of my inner world and outer world, past, present,
and future. It has helped to bring ease and grace
to help me through life's struggles.*

Chapter 16

I Like Who I Am Becoming
Marchell Coleman

I am an African American woman, never married, no children, and over fifty. At first glance, this would be an accurate description of me, but those who know me have come to understand the depth and breadth of my journey. The truth is that when someone does not know you, they tend to define you by the external, what they see, and not the real you. Yet, when you get past the outer exterior of my world, you begin to see the essence of me, what makes me laugh, makes me cry, or how I can be extremely shy around people, I don't know.

Even more, when you get closer in my inner circle, you will notice that I am self-contained, funny, focused, and ambitious. That is where you meet the real me, the spiritually conscious woman that has come to realize her worth; through some hard-won challenges, I have evolved, and I am blooming.

My journey through life reminds me of the peace lily, representing hope, death, and rebirth. I am the essence of the white bract flower within the peace lily that symbolizes surrender, letting go of the old to welcome the new. My story begins here.

I had to learn how to surrender my fear of rejection and other people's opinions of me. I used to hide behind a strong woman syndrome; I did not want to feel needy or weak. I was on the path of the independent woman, becoming self-sufficient, career-oriented, and driven.

At times it did not feel safe to embody these qualities. It was not as popular as today for women to follow their ambitions; it somehow went against that era's traditions. I was in my late 20's, and my life was not turning out like my peers, married with 1.5 children, a house, and a dog named Rover. What was becoming clear to me is, my life's narrative was going to be everything but traditional.

I did not understand why I was so driven. I was confused because what I wanted was conflicted with the direction of my life. By the time I was 27, I had completed my bachelor's degree, joined the military, on the fast track to building my career instead of a family.

A child of the late sixties, born into liberation

When I reflect on my journey, I notice how it compares with the sixties' historical facts; there seemed to be a connection. Let me explain; the sixties represented the highs and lows of change and transformation in America. It was a time of upheaval in our country and culture.

In that decade, several notable events would shape future generations to come. The world was changing, setting the stage for a significant liberation movement. Women's rights began to shift in this era. The women's liberation movement surged in the 1960s and '70s, seeking equal rights and greater personal freedom. Thus, women born in my generation and beyond would begin to experience life in a much different way. We would become the benefactors and the future torchbearers of this new foundation.

I am the daughter of parents from the deep south, Alabama, to be exact. During the sixties, Alabama played an essential role in the civic and social changes in society. My parents, and many others of their day, would witness civil unrest, protest, and the fight for equal rights. Liberation was the name of the game; black Americans in the south began to control their destiny and overcome many of the oppressive laws in our country. My parents were no different when they

168

decided to leave Alabama in 1965; and relocate to Atlanta, Georgia. Atlanta was a city that offered better career opportunities and had become a thriving city for African Americans.

I was born in Atlanta, Georgia, in 1968, the youngest of five children. Within a few years of my birth, my father purchased our first house in 1973. I remember the feeling of excitement that swept over our family. Our home was in a community where many progressive African American families had also purchased. I grew up in a close-knit family and community; this would become a significant factor in my development.

I am ambitious, resourceful, and persistent.

After high school, my life began to take shape in another way, I turned 18, and it was time to go to college. It was an expectation that you finish college, get a good job, and learn how to take care of yourself. I wanted more out of life; working in fast-food restaurants in high school also influenced my decisions. I wanted a career where I had freedom, and the labor was not so hard.

I looked forward to the next phase of my life, but I had no clue how different college would be versus high school. I feared what was ahead after graduation. Over the next ten years, I would discover many things about myself and my character.

As I reflect on my early days of college, I was immature and unprepared for the responsibilities that lie ahead. My study skills were not that strong; I was shy and was less likely to reach out to ask for help. The most challenging part was not researching careers; it was getting into college and graduating. When I got to college, it was a different experience. In classes, If you did not ask questions, it was thought that you had no problems. Conversely, If you asked questions, often, the responses would be fast and abrupt. You had to be strong mentally and emotionally, I think I was, but it would take much longer for me to catch up with the pace of the process.

When I got to the university level, the classes were huge, sometimes more than one hundred students. We packed into lecture halls with often little personal one to one attention. You were a number and last name. I felt lost and overwhelmed most of the time. The intimidation was real. I would often sit there in the class, smile, and act like I knew what was going on when I did not. Those years in college taught me a lot about persistence and commitment. It was more than just making good grades; it was about staying the course, even when everything around you said to give up and throw in the towel.

I am a college student, an overcomer, and finish what I start.

In my early college days, I did well to establish a foundation of my core courses. It was when I declared a major that kept me in a cycle of false starts and do-overs; by my sophomore year, I must have changed my major two or three times. I abandoned the physical therapy career dream early on my journey. I considered nursing, psychology, education, and even mass media communication. There were many choices, and I had no idea which road to take. But, I had this inner drive that splashed moments of inspiration when I would learn about a new career path. I would change my major or experiment with classes as electives to see if I wanted to go in one direction or another.

But little did I know all the changes and lack of focus was catching up with me. A couple of D grades got me placed on academic probation, and the final shoe dropped when I made an F or two. Then my life took an unexpected turn, and my biggest fear had come upon me. I received a letter from the university stating that I was on academic suspension for one year due to poor academic performance. The reality had set in, and I was not only unable to go back to the college that suspended me, but I also could not attend other colleges until the issue was resolved.

Through this process, I learned that helped me understand others; often, poor academic performance has very little to do with intelligence or how smart you are. It has more to do with making sure you are in the right major, have good study skills, and commit to finishing what you started. If I had to rate myself, I came to the table with one out of three. I was committed to finishing what I started. But I needed more support with the other two.

The suspension letter gave me the option to appeal the decision. At the time, I had never heard of academic suspension or an appeals process. The facts were that the grades were on my transcript, and my academic performance violated the university grade policy. I wanted to challenge the decision, but I had no fight left in me.

I resigned to my fate; it was an emotionally stressful time in my life. I felt like a failure. I wanted to believe that things would work out for my good. I am a spiritual person, so I leaned on my faith. I felt like God would put no more on me than I could handle. I wanted to believe that things would eventually get better. It felt like a thousand years had passed, and I was going nowhere fast. All I had was time on my hand; at least a year before I could apply for re-entry.

I genuinely believe that problems do not come to break us down; they make us stronger. This difficult time in my life forced me to look at the negative patterns holding me back.

I asked God to reveal what I had to do to get out of this situation. And God answered sooner than later. One morning, a few weeks after receiving the letter, I woke up with the television on, and a well-known African American motivational speaker, was on the screen. In those days, he was one of the few African Americans known in this industry. His message that day would be one of the turning points on my journey; His story was inspirational and encouraging. He had overcome many life challenges of his own.

On the same day, as I continued watching television, I experienced another breakthrough, when an infomercial featuring a professor from out of Arizona advertising a study skills program for college students. It caught my attention. The name of the program was, "Where there is a Will There is an A." In those days, our videos were on VHS tapes. This course focused on strategies to get better grades and boy did I need this program. It was like the How to's of academic success,

It was unbelievable, two miracles in one day, I got the answer to my problem. I was so excited and hopeful about the next steps. I immediately ordered the study skills program; it would become a significant turning point to transform my academic failures to success as a future honor student. When it was all said and done, it made me a better student. I was surer than ever that college was for me and that eventually, I would return, more prepared, mature, and wiser. Although this happened more than thirty years ago, it was a time of blooming for me; it was a Peace Lilly moment, the life, death, and rebirth process all at once.

I am self-aware, a believer, and determined.

During my time on academic suspension, I recognized that I had to get real with myself, look in the mirror, and ask myself some tough questions. It was a significant moment on my journey. I had created a situation, and I had to figure out how to stop it. I had to make peace with myself; I had to get on track and stay on track.

I did make some changes. I also relied on my faith more than my efforts. I recognized that it was God that led me to the solutions. It was no coincidence that I saw Motivational Speaker Les Brown on television that morning, or the professor advertising the success strategies. It was the voice of God that was leading me and guiding me the whole time.

Around the Fall of 1992, the university sent me a letter to re-enroll. I was ready. I met with the academic advisor. Before my academic suspension, academic advisement was just a formality. It was something I did because it was a part of the school policy. But this time was different. I also wanted to prove to myself and the university that I could be successful. I had declared a new major, a BA in Mental Health and Human Services. It was a time of celebration for me; it felt good. Finally, there was a clear path to work after I graduated.

One of my favorite quotes I heard in those days, "Tough times never last, but tough people do," and I became one of those tough people; As fate would have it, there were a few more twists and turns to my story. But it did not knock me down. Shortly, after re-enrolling another academic crisis was unfolding. Let me explain; the new major I had chosen was going to be grandfathered by the university. I was a few semesters shy of meeting the required timeline to stay in the program. I had to make another change. I was not alone; the school advisors and counselors were right there with me. I felt supported; I knew my options and was able to make the best decision. I was moving forward.

I would minor in Mental Health and Human Services and declare my new major, Sociology. It was the perfect setup. The decisions I made during my undergraduate journey paid off in ways I could never imagine. I know that it was God shaping my path. I was becoming more and more aligned with my career and purpose.

I have a career, I am a graduate student, and I have a mentor.

At this point on my journey, I quietly entered my 30's; I enjoyed life, having fun, dating but marriage seemed nowhere in sight. I was a shining light in my career. Although I desired more from life than a great job, it appeared marriage and children were not in the cards. Maybe God had a particular purpose in my life.

At this stage of my career, I had settled into a great job, working with an agency that allowed me to do work I loved.

I loved my career; I went to work early and left late. I made a decent salary. For me, life was good.

Soon, a new opportunity opened up in the agency. I met the qualifications. The only thing standing in the way of progress was me. I could be stubborn and obstinate about change. This new opportunity was something I always wanted to do; it was these types of next-level moves that every career-minded person dreamed.

By this time, I knew a lot more about what it meant to surrender and release control of the situation. Several months passed, and I received the promotion. I was excited about the new challenge and believed that this was a time in my life that I would begin to experience a more traditional life. I could settle down and truly focus on a relationship and live the life that I always desired. Little did I know things were about to change again.

One day, the agency director called me into her office. Ms. J. was the director and a person I had grown to trust and admire. I considered her a mentor; she was a positive light on my career journey. She had taken me under her wing and mentored me. When she called me into her office, I was not worried or had any negative thoughts about the situation.

The year was 1998, and our agency had just gone through a transition. This change in the agency's plan opened the opportunity for the new job I had just acquired. The meeting was straight forward; the director got right to the point. After congratulating me on the new promotion, she quickly shifted the conversation. She wanted to see if I had planned to go back to school to get more education. I was shocked and surprised at the direction of the conversation. I responded with a reluctant; I have not thought about it.

A few minutes later, she suggested that I consider returning to college to study for a master's degree. While I was confused about this discussion, I trusted her wisdom. Initially, I was disappointed that another level of responsibility was being placed on my shoulder. Why was I single out for this type of discussion? I knew that no other employee on the administration team had a master's degree. So many questions were running through my head.

I followed her recommendation and started my research. I researched graduate schools in my state and a few out of state. I had no idea what I would study or where to focus my next career choice. Ultimately, I chose to focus my search on a master's degree in professional counseling. It felt like a natural next level for me. I applied to a few schools and waited for a response. I had a feeling that something positive was going to happen; things were aligning perfectly. I received an acceptance letter from a university in Alabama. I was excited and nervous at the same time. Now I had two challenges to figure out. The school was about three hours away from where I lived; it was a traditional full-time program in residence.

I had to weigh my options. After some reflection, I scheduled a meeting with my director to share the updates. My director was too thrilled that I had received an acceptance letter. But I was worried, and I did not know how she would respond. Her response was positive but vague; she wanted me to continue my research.

I began immediately; to my surprise, there were some options that I was not aware of at the time of my application. I discovered the school had recently opened a satellite campus in a city closer to my home. Instead of traveling almost three hours to school, the satellite campus would take me half the time to get there. Everything was again aligning perfectly.

I enrolled and completed the master's program in less than two years without taking breaks. Despite a few bumps in the road, I graduated in two years; I passed all of my program qualification exams. I graduated with high honors; and was inducted into the Counseling National Honor Society.

I am a licensed counselor, entrepreneur, and a woman blooming.

My bloom started when I accepted that my path was going to be different. With each step on my journey, I questioned many things. At times it was not easy to accept that my life would not go the traditional route of many of my peers.

There were times when it did not feel okay to be thirty, forty, and now in my fifties, never married, no children. I also had to accept that people would not always understand why my life was going in a direction that did not fit into the traditional stereotype. Instead of seeing me for whom I was becoming, I often got sympathy or empathy as if something were wrong with my life direction.

We each have a story to tell, how we have made it this far, the challenges and wins we have experienced along the way. We each have an assignment here on earth; no two journeys are alike. Through the twist and turns of my life journey, I have come to a place of self-acceptance, seeing myself as God sees me. My work has taken me to forty-two states and three continents. My journey is not one of sacrifice but that of obedience. It was not one of giving all and receiving little in return. It is a spiritual exchange that will never dry out.

I am the sixties child, born into change, civil unrest, the women's liberation movement, and breaking down tradition, like the peace lily that symbolizes death, rebirth, hope, and surrender. I am expecting the next decades of my life to be even better than the former.

My name is Marchell Coleman, and I will BLOOM wherever I am planted.

Meet Marchell Coleman

Marchell Coleman is a Native of Atlanta Georgia, she relocated to Savannah Georgia in 2013, due to the needs of her career. Her work spans over 25 years, as a multi-passionate professional in the field of Counseling & Psychology, Life & Business Coaching. She completed her bachelor's degree in Sociology from Georgia State University in Atlanta Georgia, and Master of Science Degree in Counseling and Psychology from Troy University, Troy, Alabama. She holds quite a few credentials that have supported the success of her professional career.

She is the founder of The Divine Ambition Blueprint, a spiritually focused, divinely purposed multi passionate business that serves and supports the values of spiritually conscious highly ambitious women, that have a desire to transform their expertise gained through years of career success into a successful, financially sustainable business.

Marchell adds unique value to her work with clients, as a highly intuitive professional, she offers solutions for her clients that aligns with their personal and professional path. Her practical and down to earth approach to life helps her to remain fully engaged in the process of helping and facilitating lasting change and transformation.

Website: www.divineambitionblueprint.com
Email: contact@marchellcoleman.com

REGINA BROWN

A gardenia jasminoide represents
purity, hope and love.

The extracts from its fruit have healing properties
including anti-inflammatory, antiseptic and
antifungal effects. It is believed to help with sleep,
memory and mood problems.

As I considered a flower to represent my bloom
experience, I believe that the gardenia is most reflective
of my journey. I needed clarity along the way because I
knew that I had made a series of wrong decisions. I
needed to know where I was and how I got there. I
needed to recalculate my position in the same way that
a GPS attempts to correct a wrong turn.

Chapter 17

Gardenia Rising
Dr. Regina S. Brown

Have you ever felt nervous about sharing something about yourself because you were unsure how you would be perceived afterward? Well, that's where I find myself as I prepare to pen this story. For a variety of reasons, this part of my bloom experience was challenging to share. I am a well-educated black woman from a great family and middle-class community. I am also a clinical psychologist who is considered a subject matter expert in thoughts, feelings, behaviors, and relationships. It seems that women like me, with a so-called pedigree, would not encounter the issues that I am sharing.

This is an undeniable false expectation. For this reason, I wanted to share my experience and some of the things that I learned from it. I realize that my anxiety is stirred because I will expose some of my vulnerabilities and blind spots. I am hoping that as I share my story and the lessons that I gathered along the way, you will glean insight and wisdom that will inform your decision-making when it comes to choosing a husband.

The Dilemma

I am not the first woman, nor will I be the last who married the wrong man. This is not about accusing "Bill" (a pseudonym that I will use throughout). It is about choosing a partner who was not a good fit for me and how, consequently, that choice impacted my life for years to come.

Over twenty years ago. I relocated from my home on the East Coast to the Midwest to start working on my doctorate. I left all that was familiar behind – family, friends, church, and work. Although Chicago was an exciting city with lots to offer, as the weeks and months of the transition into full-time studies unfolded, I longed for home. I made new friends and adjusted to my environment, but I longed for comfort from the stress of rigorous academic studies and the loss of my support system.

I met Bill about six months after moving to Chicago. He was a nice guy who had also relocated to the Midwest from the Mid-Atlantic region. We developed a friendship based on our common interests and experiences. He became a good friend to me.

During his visits, Bill was supportive and caring. I recall him regularly making dinner for me as I prepared to work overnight shifts at a local hospital. He cheered me on when I struggled through challenging academic assignments. As our relationship progressed to something more serious, I started to notice things that would concern me, such as financial mismanagement or strain with his family back home. I was so focused on my academic goals that I did not pay much attention to what was going on with Bill. He was serving a purpose: companionship.

Throughout our relationship, a theme started to evolve that concerned me. Bill was friendly and engaging, but he had difficulty with problem-solving and working through conflicts. He would see himself as the victim in professional and personal situations when a comprehensive review of the circumstances would suggest otherwise. Sometimes, his narrative was so left of center; I felt sorry for him. I would voice my concerns about his skewed perspective and provide him with alternate viewpoints to help him navigate his issues.

Despite this, Bill's good outweighed his bad, so the relationship continued to deepen, and we eventually married. However, there was no blissful honeymoon phase because Bill quit his job four weeks before we tied the knot. He was unhappy at work and abruptly resigned, although he agreed to be the sole breadwinner while completing my doctoral studies. Bill did not have a job when we married. He was also not leaving one job for another. He had no Plan B.

Our marriage started with financial strain as we used monetary wedding gifts to pay essential expenditures like rent. I began to feel resentment because of his impulsivity and irresponsibility. I started working part-time and tabled my academic pursuits.

All the while, Bill made minimal efforts to rectify the financial downturn we were experiencing. On the surface, things seemed to stabilize, but there was a growing disconnection between us. By the time I graduated, we were "married singles." Bill spent more and more time away from home, and I was adjusting to life without doctoral studies' rigors.

The more that I tried to reconnect with Bill, the further away he seemed to be. He spent his days playing video games, watching television, and eating takeout. He stopped attending church and no longer participated in small group exercises. I sought counsel from friends, pastors, therapists (as a client, not a colleague), and even our parents, but Bill was unresponsive to all efforts. He made it clear that he wanted to be on his own, and the discovery of multiple extramarital affairs confirmed this. We divorced less than four years into our marriage.

I was heartbroken when our marriage ended. I struggled with grief and shame that something I wanted for so long had nosedived. However, if I am honest with myself, our marriage was destined to fail from the beginning because I did not pick well.

Lessons from the heart: Self-examination

The most painful lesson was realizing that I had brought this situation on myself because many of the issues manifested in our marriage were evident earlier on in the relationship. I did not wake up one morning and find myself in an unhealthy marriage. I made several conscious decisions along the way that lead up to that point.

In graduate school, I experienced some of the darkest days of my life. The academic rigor, for the most, was expected. However, the social disconnection and isolation that I experienced were not. I was one of very few students of color in my cohort and the only black person in most of my classes. I lived in an area where most people did not look like me and did not share my sociopolitical views. I felt very alone. Emotionally, I started to falter and was having difficulty hearing from God during that season.

The fruit that I was bearing in my life during that season, anxiety, weariness, and frustration would be prominent. It was clear that my life led me away from the familiar to start a new chapter. I did not realize the process would be disorienting and frightening at times. So, in desperation, I picked but did not choose wisely. Years ago, Lauren Hill posed a question in her well-known song, "How you gonna win when you ain't right within?" I did not pick well because I was not in a healthy place.

Yes, I was a therapist and an emerging psychologist. I was also a woman who was in a vulnerable place in her journey. I was not thinking clearly. I stayed in an unhealthy situation to my demise, and it derailed my life for years.

For me, hope was a significant factor in why I decided to stick with the wrong partner. I had invested time, emotions, and energy in the relationship. I wanted a return on my investment. Bill had the potential to become who I wanted him to be. I hoped that he would grow beyond any of his issues and that we could grow together as a couple. As I focused on what was lacking in the relationship, I became more and more dissatisfied.

I knew that the chance of ending the relationship would mean that I would have to start all over again with someone else. I was also aware of the statistics regarding a black woman's chances of finding a partner. Supposedly, that chance decreases with every educational degree that she earns. I felt that it was best to work with the man I already had rather than cutting bait.

Lessons from the orchard: "Never listen to what the tree says. Judge it by its fruit."

In the Bible, Jesus warned his followers not to be deceived by the outward appearance of false prophets but rather to judge a tree by its fruit. In Matthew 7:16-19, we find the following admonition: "You will recognize them by their fruits. Are grapes gathered from thornbushes or figs from thistles? So, every healthy tree bears good fruit, but the diseased tree bears bad fruit. A healthy tree cannot bear bad fruit, nor can a diseased tree bear good fruit. Every tree that does not bear good fruit is cut down and thrown into the fire. Thus, you will recognize them by their fruits." In the same way that Jesus provided a framework for detecting the validity of prophets, it is vital to use that same wisdom in determining the constitution of potential partners.

Jesus' framework suggests that there can only be three outcomes when considering a tree's productivity: good fruit, bad fruit, and no fruit. If a tree is personified under examination, it can come up with various reasons to explain the condition of the fruit it bears. Indeed, if the fruit is on the level of or exceeds expectations, then there is no problem. This tree is determined to have good fruit. When asked, that tree can confidently present it produce. However, if the quality and quantity of its fruit are not up to par (bad or nonexistent), the tree may explain its productiveness with the following statements:

"Another tree is shading me. If the sun shone directly on me, I would have produced better fruit."

185

"The aphids, caterpillars, and beetles attacked me and impacted my productivity."

"It does not rain enough. My soil is dry."

"People keep carving their initials into my trunk. That is disrespectful and upsetting. I cannot grow in conditions like this."

Often, the tree's narrative regarding its substandard productivity will expose underlying issues. Some of those issues may reveal difficulties with accountability and stewardship. In the same way, partners may rationalize or justify their lack of growth (or fruitfulness) in areas essential for a productive life and healthy relationship.

Although I had some concerns about things that I observed in Bill's life, it was a mistake to discuss it with him because he had several compelling reasons for rationalizing his state of affairs. He was unwavering about how he had been mistreated and undermined at various times of his life. These issues moved me, and I felt compassion for him. I did not want to become another person who wounded him. My compassion eclipsed common sense. As time passed, I realized that Bill was not growing from those experiences and had settled into the victim's role. His growth was stunted, and ultimately, I was stunted.

Lessons from the pantry: "Spam versus filet mignon"

Typically, crises drive me to my knees in prayer. As the marriage was crumbling, I sought divine insight into my situation. I remember God telling me that I could not expect filet mignon if I started with Spam. It was a simple metaphor with a strong message—ingredients matter. If you are a foodie like I am, you know that a meal's outcome is directly related to the ingredients selected from the onset. This concept is also true when picking a partner.

I did not marry a man consistent with the qualities that I desired in a lifelong partner. He was fun, friendly, and supportive. I needed that in a friend. Yet he was never

186

supposed to be more than that. I had compromised because I was more invested in his potential than accepting his reality. I knew that there were some character issues that I found troubling, but I did not have the courage, energy, or focus to do what I needed to do. I did not want to endure a painful breakup, so I went along to get along. The thing that I avoided – a breakup – ended up with a much worse result – divorce.

Lessons from the closet: "Compelled to control."

There was a protracted time in our marriage where Bill had disconnected and was doing his own thing. He stopped letting me know when he was coming home from work and disappeared most weekends without accountability. When he was home, we did not interact much. As we settle into being married singles, I felt abandoned in the effort to save our marriage.

I found solace in my walk-in closet. This is where I prayed and had hushed conversations with my family and closest friends. My support group provided much-need insight and wisdom along the way.

Why did I do this? Why did I invest in someone who was not a good fit for me? Why did I blaze through red flags as if they did not provide warning that danger was ahead?

Although I saw many of the issues ahead of time, I felt that somehow things would change. When Bill was not growing in the areas that I desired, I pressured him to conform to the image I wanted. I was encouraging initially, but I often spoke up when there was little productivity in his life. This frustrated him because he knew that I wanted more, and he was not up to the task.

Essentially, I was communicating that he was not up to par. Conversely, I cannot imagine what that stirred in him. If you have ever been in a situation where you felt that you were not good enough for your partner, it has to be a painful experience. He was not designed to be with me; neither was

I supposed to be with him. It was like trying to fit a square peg in a round hole.

What do I want the next generation to know?

Do not make significant decisions in your love life while going through a significant transition. Change requires emotional, cognitive, and spiritual resources that can be stretched and strained during these times. Transitions can be stressful and taxing, making you more emotionally vulnerable than usual. "Friend Zone" everyone until your judgment is clear.

Know your vulnerabilities and blind spots because that may determine what kind of fruit you are prone to pick. Many women are socialized to be nurturers and helpers. You may be drawn to those who need assistance. Persons who are called to healing professions or ministries may be drawn to those who are wounded.

There is some truth to the "opposites attract" adage. However, it is crucial to determine what that relationship should be once you have examined a person's fruit. Some people should be our patients and not our partners. Going back to Jesus' admonition in Matthew 7, we see that there are only three outcomes: good fruit, bad fruit, and no fruit.

Take time to evaluate the fruit in a potential partner's life thoroughly. Look at their patterns. Check out their past. Find out who is in their circle. These factors will give you a more in-depth insight into that person's fruit and their constitution. You want to know to make your decision about their goodness-of-fit for your life based on that. If you are distracted like I was, it is easy to become attached to the waxy, bright side of a person while not properly evaluating their hidden, moldy parts. They may look healthy from one perspective, but closer examination may reveal a discolored, faded, or rotten side that is out of view. Make your choice based on the quality of the fruit and not just the outward appearance. Pick well.

We do not want to rake potential partners over the coals because they are not where we want them to be. I suggest that a standard is set and upheld when it comes to what we expect out of a partner. If you prematurely commit, there is no guarantee that they will ever produce the fruit we hope.

Be clear on what role you want to assume in your relationship. Move away from situations that cast you in the role of a project manager responsible for the relationship's entire scope. If the relationship's success or failure rests solely on your shoulders, you will over-function and end up over-burdened. Marriage is a partnership of individuals who assume various responsibilities that can change over time. Make sure there is a balance in the partnership that you establish.

I cannot emphasize this enough - do not compromise your standards. If you want fruit consistent with responsibility, integrity, loyalty, and kindness, wait for it to be demonstrated before committing yourself. Essentially, do not pick fruit before it is ripe. Let maturity become evident. Growth and productivity are essential to any healthy relationship.

It is okay to walk away from individuals whose fruit are substandard. Lack of fruitfulness can indicate deficits in integrity, dedication, transparency, and loyalty. This can come at a high price down the road. It is okay to let people go to free up space in your heart and mind for the right person.

When things do not work out as expected, there is a tendency to deconstruct all of the factors involved to identify the root cause of failure. That is a natural response. Process your feelings but do not get stuck in rehearsing the "what ifs" of the situation. A bad pick will always be a bad pick. No amount of contemplation will change that. Grieve, identify the lessons, and move forward.

Give someone that you trust access to your relationship so that they can tell you hard truths. If you incline to pick poorly, you may want to appoint someone who knows you well to be a quality assurance manager. Their job is to provide you with honest feedback about your pick. Trust them. They can see beyond the blinding giddiness of infatuation and love.

My name is Dr. Regina S. Brown, and I will continue to BLOOM wherever I am planted.

Reference:

Hill, L. (1998). Doo Wop (That Thing) [Recorded by L. Hill]. On *The Miseducation of Lauryn Hill*. Kingston, Jamaica: Marley Music, Inc.

Meet Regina Brown

Dr. Regina S. Brown is a Licensed Psychologist and Licensed Professional Counselor with over 25 years of experience in behavioral health. She holds two master's degrees (one in Counseling, the other in Theology) as well as a Doctorate in Clinical Psychology. She has worked in a variety of settings including residential treatment homes, child development centers, nursing homes, detention centers, churches and schools.

She is an expert in conducting psychological evaluations and has used her skills in forensic inquiries for court systems and fitness for duty cases with the VA, Social Security and a number of other agencies. Dr. Brown has served as a behavioral health consultant for schools and organizations and has facilitated presentations and leadership trainings for various groups. She has extensive training in military psychology and has worked for the Department of Defense where she served Veterans, active duty service members and their families.

Her professional interests include clergy mental health, phase-of-life issues, neuropsychology, trauma processing and immigration/acculturation issues. She enjoys working with diverse clientele and is passionate about de-stigmatizing mental health conditions within communities of color.

Website: www.transitionspsych.org
Email: drreginasbrown@gmail.com

RETTA SMITH

A red ginger is an exotic flower that represents fiery passion and strength.

During this time of sheltering in place, I have been observing the flowers on my patio. I noticed when I got out early in the morning, the blooms are shut. As the morning gets warmer and the sun comes out, they slowly unfold, opening their face to be kissed by the sun as approval to carry on with their day.

The Red Ginger is no different it thrives in hit hot temperatures. Although it blooms and flowers year-round, the blooms are the prettiest during the summer heat. Much like my story. Like the red ginger, my dream unfolded like the Red Ginger through some of the hottest trials of my life.

193

Chapter 18

JOURNEY TO A DREAM
Barbarette "Retta" Smith

The journey to my dream began in August 2000. It was around the time my youngest son left for college. I was now an empty nester, and it was my time to do something for me for a change. I vividly remember the day I took him to college and the ride home as if it was yesterday. I cried all the way home. Tears I had held back for most of his senior year as I encouraged and pushed him to prepare for college.

The focus of my adult life was poured into raising my son's, preparing them to be Black men in a challenging world. Every fall was football. Every winter was basketball, and every spring was baseball. Summers were focused on finding practical educational activities to keep them focused and busy while I worked. I focused on preparing them for success.

All of these memories flooded my mind on that ride home. I am generally not someone who does a lot of crying, but memories and tears flowed uncontrollably. This was the end of a season in my life. I felt lost. I felt afraid. I had questions about what was next for me. I knew I didn't want to be one of those mothers who felt their life was over. I had a lot to offer, but how? Where?

I began to reflect on some of the questions we are asked in elementary school: "What do you want to be when you grow up?" I recalled I had a dream of being a nurse or a psychiatrist. All my high school course electives were directed toward preparing me to be a nurse: psychology, chemistry, physiology, and science. I knew pursuing a career as a psychiatrist was a long shot because that would require going to school for a long time, which was against my family's norms. College was seen as a waste of time and money when you could be working. As I was thinking and reflecting, I decided on a counselor, a therapist—it was time to research.

A little about me: I grew up as an only child in a single-parent household with my mother and aunt. I was close to my father, but he and my mother were divorced. He lived down the street, so he wasn't an absent father, but my mother raised me.

As an only child, I spent a lot of time reading. I always read about people leaving home and going away to college. A dream I knew, for me, was a long shot. I grew up in a blue-collar town where success to black folks was to get a good-paying job in one of the local factories; or go to a vocational school and get a good-paying job working in the local factory. Along the way, I got married and had two sons. I went from my mother's house to becoming a wife and later a mother. The possibility of going to college was now farther away. It was just that, a dream.

I was either married or a single parent during my adult life, always putting everyone else needs before mine.

Eventually, I did fulfill my dream of going to college part-time. I was able to maintain my job and focused on raising my boys. There were several people close to me with a different opinion. I started at the local Junior college. I would attend college at night after I got off work. Later a non-traditional program offered weekend courses.

My husband was totally against me going to college. We got a divorce during this time. It was hard working full time and going to school part-time with little or no support from anyone emotionally or financially. Family and friends use to ridicule me for going to school when I already had a decent paying job. But I wanted more. I wanted to love my job; I also wanted one of the jobs I read about, a house and to travel to exotic places.

It took over ten years for me to get my undergraduate degree in Business Administration. It was the fastest route to a degree. Through the non-traditional program, I was able to use my work experience toward college credits. I earned 30 credit hours, the maximum credits the program offered, for my work experience. The lesson in this is God can and will use anything to move you forward.

Now it was my time to live and pursue my dreams. At this time, I had moved to Bloomington from my hometown. While actively working in ministry, one of the things I noticed the need for mental health counseling.

My dream to become a counselor/ therapist was once again awakened, but I didn't want to be an ordinary counselor. I wanted to be a Christian counselor because the word of God heals. God is the great healer, Jehovah Rapha. Although I wanted to be a Christian counselor, this still required a graduate degree. The thought of going back to school while working toward a degree was not appealing. My recollection of past challenging experiences in school flooded back. I did not share this with anyone. I needed a plan.

I was still thinking, pondering, and reflecting on whether I should pursue or do something similar that didn't require more schooling. Something that wouldn't be so difficult to accomplish. One thing I have learned over time is, when God puts a desire in your heart, it is a done deal. He won't let it go and will give you what you need to get you to the next step. He promised, *"And I am sure of this, that he who began a good work in you will bring it to completion at the day of Jesus Christ"* Philippians 1:6 (ESV).

After a women's prayer event at church, one of our intercessors, Sis. Dean approached me about something the Lord gave her to share with me. I was nervous and shaking because I knew this little, but mighty God's woman hears from the Lord. What she told me had a lasting impact, and it is still unfolding today 20+ years later. She shared the scripture the Lord had given her for me, *"Blessed is the man who walks not in the counsel of the wicked, nor stands in the way of sinners, nor sits in the seat of scoffers; but his delight is in the law of the Lord, and his law he meditates day and night"* (Psalm 1:1).

She told me, "the Lord was leading me to help others through Counseling. I was to study His word and that He would order my steps. She said I would dream dreams and write books. She told me a book was forming on the inside of me, and she saw me standing before an audience of people sharing His word. People would be healed and set free." I am sure she said more, but that's all I could handle at the time. Remember, God gives you what you need for the next step...what I got out of all was confirmed to return to school. It had settled. I was going back to school to get a master's degree in counseling. I had no idea what a journey that would be.

Thank God He only gives us a glimpse of what He has called us to do and not the full picture. I can relate my life to one of my daily devotions, "There Is More in You" from Bishop T.D. Jakes, "He knew before you were formed what you would be. Everything in your life is shaping your destiny. Much like God, what you are going to be is hidden in what you are and what you were."

Since I was moving from Business Administration to Psychology, I wanted to find a college without completing an undergraduate degree in Psychology or a lot of prerequisites. Also, where I could attend while working full time. My search turned out to be relatively easy. I just knew this was a sign of things to come, little did I know this was far from the truth.

I ran into a couple of friends who wanted to pursue a counseling degree to support their business. There are no coincidences in the plan of God. He's always ordering our steps. They were already attending counseling classes at the University of Illinois – Springfield.

It was about an hour commute to class. We agreed to carpool. The perfect arrangement. Friends riding to school together, studying together, and saving on gas. Everything was falling into place. I was on my way to fulfilling my lifelong dream of becoming a counselor. Once I heard a preacher say, "Any dream you can accomplish on your own without God's help is a man-made dream." God was getting ready to show me this dream was a God-given dream and that I would need Him for it to come to past.

One of my first obstacles, the friends I started with, quit after the three semesters. Now I was alone on my journey driving to class after work two-three times a week for a three-hour class. Some nights, I would get home close to 11:00 pm. It was difficult. I had done this before and felt I could do it again. The difference this time around was I had remarried and again no support. As a matter of fact, in addition to the lack of support from home, our marriage was struggling. Isn't it ironic that I am pursuing a counseling degree with a marriage and family focus, and my marriage was failing?

Everything in me began to question, "Is this what God was saying?" Doubt started to creep in. I prayed and asked God, "What should I do?" Silence. Another lesson I learned during this difficult time was to keep it moving. Keep pursuing the dream until God says, "No." Go back to the promise. Go back to scriptures that motivated me to begin. I began to meditate on them daily. That was the difference this time. I grew closer to God and felt Him carrying me through it all.

It usually takes full time students two years to finish practicum and internship it took me four years to complete attending parttime. Working fulltime made it challenging to find an agency where I could get my required number of individual and group counseling hours. I had to intern at two agencies to meet curriculum hour requirements. In essence, I was working a full-time job, two part-time jobs, working

Beginning my last year of internship, my full-time job had a lot of leadership turnover. I was asked to go to Dallas, TX, to work for 90 days until they could fill certain positions. I had a dilemma. How would I finish this last semester of school while working in Dallas? The Bible says in James 4:2

(ESV), *"We have not because we ask not."* I presented a proposal to my leadership listing conditions under which I would go. God worked it out to come home for class once every three weeks to meet with my professor to fulfill the Internship course requirements.

At the end of my 90-day assignment, I was offered a management position. It was an opportunity to escape the relationship drama, big promotion, and the prospect to start over in an exciting city where no one knew me. I would oversee a department of 26 people. Something I had always wanted to do but didn't think was possible. I thought this must be from God. Although at the back of my mind I was thinking, "Are you willing to give up all you worked for this position?" I prayed—nothing from God.

I was given a few days to make a decision about the position. Man's timeline does not move God. Still nothing. I accepted the position, but I had no peace. I cried all the time when people would say, "Congratulations! Well deserved! We are so happy for you!" Instead of saying, "Thank you." A pain would well up in my chest, my breath would get short, and tears would flow down my face. Such a disconnect from what I thought was an opportunity of a lifetime. I was supposed to be happy, overjoyed. And planning my big move to Dallas. Still no answer from God.

One of my Dallas co-workers took me to church with her to Wednesday night Bible study at the Potter's House. There was a guest speaker, Bishop John Frances. He preached a message: "Curse It! It's a Deception!" from Mark 11:12-24. Immediately, something in my spirit jumped. I got lightheaded; my heart started racing, and tears started flowing like a river. I am surprised that I could take notes. I heard the Lord say, "Listen, this is your answer." I knew from the title of the message that whatever was coming would be challenging but life changing.

Bishop Frances said, "He was talking to someone who had made some decisions they had to go back and correct. He said I don't know who it is. I think it is a job or a move or something. You need to go back and correct it."

I knew it was me I had to go back and retract my agreement to accept the position. I had to go home and deal with some things. Speak to some things to change the trajectory of my life. I went back and told my boss I couldn't accept the position and returned home. I knew when I got home; my marriage would be over. I remember everything just like it was yesterday. When I reflect on this time, I can still see Bishop Frances delivering that word. God had something greater in store for me.

The next lesson learned, when encountering conflicting opinions or decisions, it is good to remember that *"For God is not a God of confusion but peace"* (1 Corinthians 14:33). Trust what God has said, no matter how it looks. No matter the circumstances. He knows our future and orders our steps.

The next year was challenging; every obstacle I faced, I knew God was with me, and He was walking beside me as I held onto the word I received. My prayer life changed, My teaching changed, and My intimacy with God increased. Looking back over this time, I realized this was necessary for God to use me in counseling.

My divorce was painful and very public. I later realized the public needed to see what I wouldn't say. I refused to chase a lie because God fought for me. This scripture carried me through it all. Psalms 27:13-14 (KJV), *"I had fainted, unless I had believed to see the goodness of the Lord in the land of the living. 14 Wait on the Lord: be of good courage, and he shall strengthen thine heart: wait, I say, on the Lord."* Not only did it bless me, but it also blessed others. I quoted it every chance I got to teach or share my testimony. He opened doors and created opportunities only He could do. That part of my life is another chapter. I want to focus on the dreams He placed in me and how they came to pass.

As I got closer and closer to completing my course requirements, I encountered more obstacles. I lost my academic advisor, the faculty changed, and an increase in course curriculum and course requirements were implemented. But God! He continued to open doors for me.

By God's grace, I finished school and graduated with my Master of Arts degree in Human Development Counseling. It took eight years from beginning to end. Hallelujah! Praise God! I did it! I now had my degree in Counseling in hand. I never use to celebrate myself, but I threw myself a graduation party. Another lesson I learned, celebrate you! I thought the hard part was over.

Now it was time to activate the dream. With my academic advisor gone, I had little to no guidance on what to do next. I felt stuck. I began to pray, "Lord, I know you didn't bring me this far to leave me. Where do I go from here?" As God would have it, I ran into someone at a community event that had completed the same program I had been in. She showed me how to get my counseling license and what to do next. I needed to take the National Counseling Exam, which comprised everything I learned over the past eight years. I studied for a few months. I took the test and failed by twelve points. My God! Help! I felt defeated. This exam was expensive! My prayer partner, Pat, offered to help me study. We would walk, and she would quiz me. We did this for months as I saved up to retake the exam. Little did she know, deep down inside, I wasn't going to take that exam. I was done!

Our church went to the Spirit and Truth Conference at New Birth Missionary Baptist Church in Atlanta, Georgia. I remember Bishop Neil Ellis preaching about "The Anointing." He had an altar call for us to receive a fresh anointing. Of course, I went. I needed to hear something from the Lord. He was still silent.

That next morning the Lord woke me up, and I began to write. If I could capture what He said in one phrase, it would be, "You Dream Too Small." He laid out the vision for me as it related to my dream of being a counselor. I would not be

202

just a counselor, so I started my own business, private practice. It blew my mind.

Seriously, God? I don't have a license to do any of this; you are talking about starting a business! There was not one thing in what He shared I felt I could do. My dream of becoming a counselor was too small. I was reminded of the difference between a man-made dream and a God-dream. Now my dream was a God-dream. I was refreshed, renewed, and motivated to resume studying for the exam.

When we got back from Atlanta, Bishop Taylor said, "It's time to license my ministers and teachers." He told me I was one of the people God said would be selected to receive a ministerial license. A minister's license. I thought I was getting a license in Counseling. I heard a small whisper from the Lord, "Christian Counselor." I was getting my credentialing in the spirit and didn't even know it. Praise God!

Now onto the natural. Pat and I continued to pray, and we studied up to the day before my scheduled exam. I went into that exam with the strength and confidence of God. Six weeks later, I got the notice in the mail; I passed with flying colors! I know my neighbors probably thought I got some bad news in the mail. I stood at the mailbox, crying and giving God glory and praise. I was overwhelmed with His love. I immediately applied for my license and received them in the mail within weeks.

I got my degree and license. Now I moved on to research for the business. I was directed to Faye Freeman- Smith, the Counseling Director at the local Community College in my research. After a few years of supervision and mentoring, I opened my business: Rophe Place (The Healing Place) Counseling Services on September 1, 2014. I had one client, and I was scared and ecstatic at the same time.

Over the past few years, I have seen nothing but blessings and blessings. One of my greatest blessings is my husband, James L. Smith; he is a mighty man of God. He is my best friend, confidant, and partner in all things. He pushes me toward my destiny when I want to give up and settle for less. He is the deep voice that says, "Is that what God would want you to do?" He supports me in prayer and encouragement. We facilitate pre-marital Counseling together. I am in tears just thinking about him and looking back over my life if I stayed in Dallas, TX. I wouldn't have ever met him. Our paths would have never crossed.

In June of 2019, I retired from my full time Corporate job of 30 years to work private practice. I started with one client and now I have over 25+ clients and growing daily. Some clients specifically ask if I am a Christian Counselor, and would I pray with them. I am so grateful for how God is working in my life. This journey to a dream has taken over 20 years to bloom into who God said I would become. God is still moving and working on my behalf, just like He said he would. He loves us and wants the best for us. Jeremiah 29:11, *"For I know the plans I have for you, declares the Lord, plans for welfare and not for evil, to give you a future and a hope."*

Just like the red ginger, I tend to thrive best in hot and humid conditions. God is using me to help bring healing to not only common concerns such as anxiety, depression, and anger management. He is also using me to bring about clarity and peace in life-changing situations, such as relationships, conflict, divorce, and grief.

My name is Retta Smith, and I will continue to BLOOM wherever I am planted.

Meet Retta Smith

Barbarette Smith, affectionally known as "Retta" is a Licensed Professional Counselor, Bible Teacher and Workshop Facilitator. She holds a bachelor's degree in Business Administration and a second Bachelor's in Theology. Her Master's Degree is in Human Development Counseling.

Retta has a gifting and passion for teaching. She has facilitated numerous parenting, leadership and personal development workshops in the community, corporate settings and churches. In 2008, Retta was afforded the opportunity to expand her love for teaching internationally. As a Licensed Minister and Bible Teacher, she traveled abroad with her church to train and teach audiences in South Africa and the Dominican Republic.

After retiring from a 30-year corporate career, Retta recently fulfilled her dream of starting a business. She established, Rophe Place, a counseling practice geared towards addressing the emotional and spiritual needs of hurting people.

Retta is married to James Smith, they have three sons and five grandchildren.

RICHETTA PORTER

*A daisy represents innocence,
purity, rebirth and newness.*

*The daisy knows what it can bring to the world even
when the world doesn't think it brings any value.*

*Daisies are so common that they are over-looked and
sometimes viewed as invasive. The Daisy does not care
that it is thought to be invasive intrusive. In certain
garden settings it grows in full sun, well-drained soils
and requires low to no maintenance to bring value as a
colorful ground cover. The Daisy is so unique that it
knows the importance of getting a good night sleep and
wake up when the sun rises.*

*In the days of old, it was said that when you go to bed
early you will wake up "Fresh as a Daisy."*

Chapter 19

Pretty Everlasting
Richetta Porter

It's not what you are that holds you back. It's what you think you are not that holds you back.

Have you ever felt as though your imperfection hides the best part of you? As far back as I can remember, I was always the one who was alone with my thoughts, interest, and insecurities. As the middle child of three children, I felt that it was easy to be overlooked, especially with my speech impairment. I have this condition called "Lazy Tongue."

I was so insecure when I had to speak that I hated to hear someone ask me, "What did you say? or I'm sorry, I did not hear what you said." Maybe they did, or perhaps they didn't, it bothers me the same. When I started attending middle school, my teachers would force me to speak more by reading aloud in class. You know, that exercise the teacher encouraged in the classroom? You either raised your hand or you were called upon to read out loud. Well, it seems to me that I was always the one called upon and I would not say I liked it.

My speech problem was exposed; this was hard to overcome. I tried to overshadow my speech problem with a smart mouth. I was that person who always had something smart to say to make others feel stupid and make me feel in control of the situation. I now realize that smart mouth was my insecurity manifesting.

I am like the Daisy that grows in full sun, I would practice reading at home and at school to avoid sounding as though I had cotton in my mouth. As I began to educate myself on how to exercise my tongue, I trained my tongue to pronounce my words without the cotton sound. By conquering the ability to sound somewhat normal, this encouraged me to never settle for what I do not like. Solutions applied to situations you do not like may very well change your life and help you to see your value. A daisy never stops offering to the world what it was designed to provide because it does not look like a flower with value.

What do you do when your imperfections are not so easy to change? As a teenager, I would do just about anything to fit in with my peers. I smoked cigarettes, weed, skipped school, etc. My best friend gave me the nickname "Bones." I hated it but allowed her to call me "Bones" to fit in. Then everybody in school started calling me "Bones," I felt that it was much easier to call me "Bones" than to remember my legal name. Back in 1977-1979, most of the high school girls had bodies that were well developed except for mines. They had bodies like a brick house. There was a song that came out called "Brick House." It talked about girls' bodies being shaped like a Coke Cola bottle, letting it all hang out. But for me, I did not have that problem.

One day my best friend and I were hanging out with some other friends, and someone asked me, "How did you get the name "Bones?" Before I could answer that question, my best friend spoke up and said, "Isn't it obvious?" For the first time, I felt that the sun was so bright on me, it woke me up from this deep sleep, and I realized just how my best friend felt about me. The name said it all, "Bones." At that moment, I was so upset that I allowed people to call me "Bones," but most importantly, I would answer to that name. I would say to myself, "How could I be so stupid to acknowledge that this was okay." I was on a mission to change the way others saw me, especially my so-called best friend. I would buy the padded bras, the panties with pad for the butt, and hips.

Eventually, I decided that I was going to save my money to have implant surgery. I was going to show everyone that I am no longer a little girl but a brick house.

When I started attending college, I met someone who also desired to have implant surgery. They shared with me some of the places to have the surgery performed and the cost. I was so excited that I met them; it made me feel that I was getting closer to making my dream come true of being the woman nobody would laugh at, I thought. But I would soon realize that a quick fix to anyone or anything can be dangerous.

The person I met in college went on to have the implant surgery during one summer break but did not survive the surgery. They had a heart attack during the surgery. After hearing what happen, it was like the sun woke me up out of my sleep of revenge. I was consumed with changing my body to show my peers that I can be pretty, but I could not see that I was already pretty. I remember years ago when I would hear these words being spoken over me, "You are pretty, smart and talented."

Somehow, I pushed it so far back in my subconscious mind that it took the tragedies of another to see my truth. Changing how I wish to be accepted by others never ends well. Embracing my imperfections, whether I can improve them or not, is the beginning of true self-love. I was so focused on how I sounded and how I looked that I could not see my real purpose. My imperfections were blocking me from seeing the value I would bring to the world. I realized that some imperfections may never change but can be improved while others will change over time.

In 1987, I gave birth to my first child, and after the nine months' experience of caring for a child, my body developed into a brick house naturally. It is not about how you look or how you are received by others that makes you valuable but how you are. Learning to be the best version of yourself early in your life is a GIFT. It saves you from wasting a lot of time

211

so that you can get busy making the difference you were born to make.

The world would have you to believe that there is a group of people that is perfect. But NOBODY is perfect. Everybody has imperfections. Despite your imperfections, know that you are enough. Nothing needs to be added to you, and nothing needs to be taken from you. You are perfect the way you are. Greatness is inside of you; therefore, focus on what you do well and BLOOM.

Today, I own a successful day spa in Kansas City, Missouri. As a Spa Owner and Licensed Esthetician, it is my purpose in life to serve my clients in a way that brings out the best qualities in them, and I would not have been able to do this trying to fit in. I have learned in observing the Daisy that no matter how you perceive it, it does not discount its value. That is why the Daisy is "Pretty Everlasting."

My name is Richetta Porter, and I will continue to BLOOM, where I am planted.

Meet Richetta Porter

Richetta is the owner of DeVyne Spa, a waxing parlor that provides skincare services for men, women and teens located in downtown Kansas City. Her motto is "Show Others How To Treat You By How Well You Take Care of Yourself."

Richetta is a Licensed Esthetician/Nail Technician. She started her career in the beauty industry right out of high school, landing a job as a make-up artist with the Jones Store. She went on to have a modeling career, modeling for Macy's and Chevrolet and as a runway model for Artline Agency of Kansas City.

A serial entrepreneur, Richetta has established several businesses over the years including a Secretarial Service, Cleaning Service and a Fragrance Scent Shop

Richetta is a native of Kansas City, MO, a mother of four beautiful adult children and a grandmother of five amazing grandchildren.

Website: www.Devynespa.com
Telephone: (816) 472-7779

VERNELL SCOTT

A huff lantana represents rigor. They are appreciated because they are easy to grow and thrive in most soil conditions.

I chose the Lantana – because that perennial is resilient, it can take a licking and still come up every year. The Lantana is considered toxic It is not indestructible, but unless you pull it out of the ground, it simply hangs on for dear life.